Betty Crocker's

COOKING
WITH
KIDS

Shawyn Mattox

Katie Mickelson

Jared Sanders

Adam Simonett

Jenna Gutzwiller

Jamie Ahrndt

Leslie Dolland

Max Corcoran

Rachel Jensen

Maggie Carlson

Jessie Hemp

Dan Mattison

Betty Crocker's

COOKING WITH KIDS

MACMILLAN • USA

MACMILLAN
A Simon & Schuster Macmillan Company
15 Columbus Circle
New York, NY 10023

MACMILLAN is a registered trademark of Macmillan, Inc.
BETTY CROCKER, BISQUICK, and GOLD MEDAL are registered trademarks of
General Mills, Inc.

Library of Congress Cataloging-in-Publication Data

Crocker, Betty.
[Cooking with kids]
Betty Crocker's cooking with kids.
p. cm.
Rev. ed. of: Betty Crocker's new boys' & girls' cookbook. © 1990.
Includes index.
1. Cookery—Juvenile literature. [1. Cookery.] I. Title.
TX652.5.C76 1995
651.5'123—dc20
94-24259 CIP AC

ISBN: 0-02-860363-X

GENERAL MILLS, INC.
Betty Crocker Food and Publications Center
Director: Marcia Copeland
Editor: Karen Couné
Food Stylists: Katie W. McElroy, Cindy Lund
Nutrition Department
Nutritionist: Elyse A. Cohen, M.S.
Photographic Services
Photographer: Carolyn Luxmoore

For consistent baking results, the Betty Crocker Food and Publications Center
recommends Gold Medal flour.

Manufactured in the United States of America
10 9 8 7 6 5 4 3 2 1
First Edition
Cover (left to right): Very Vegetable Soup (page 102),
Oven-Fried Chicken (page 118), Chocolate Chip Cookies (page 155),
Very Strawberry Soda (page 72), Hungry-time Hoagies (page 89)

Contents

Introduction

Welcome to a cookbook made just for you! It's full of delicious recipes and it's easy to use. All of the recipes were tested by kids so you can be sure that they really work and that they taste great.

It's always neat to learn something new, and cooking is a skill that's twice as fun because you get to eat what you make. You'll be eager to get into the kitchen and try recipes like Big Puffy Pancake, Oh-So-Chocolate Brownies, Frozen Tropical Dream Pops, One-Pot Spaghetti and Chocolate Malt Cakes. The list goes on with recipes for breakfast, lunch, dinner and snacks. We've even included plans for special occasions— after the game, a sleep over, Halloween and Mother's Day.

Before you start, be sure to read through the Cook's Corner to learn what you need to know to cook wisely and safely. It also shows you the kitchen equipment you will need and explains cooking words that may be new to you. Also, be sure to have an adult read the section just for them, "For the Cook's Adult Helper."

Always ask an adult any questions you have before you start to cook. In some of the recipes you'll see the words **Adult help**. It's especially important to let your adult helper know when you are making those recipes so they will be around to help where the recipe calls for them.

Have fun, be creative, try something new and be proud of yourself, for you're learning something that you can enjoy all your life!

Betty Crocker

Cook's Corner

Let's Get Started!

Before You Start

- Check with an adult to make sure it's a good time to make a recipe. Always let an adult know when your recipe uses the range (stove top) or oven.

- If your hair is long, tie it back so it won't get in the way.

- Wash your hands and put on an apron.

- Read the recipe all the way through before you start to cook. Ask an adult about anything you don't understand.

- Gather all the ingredients and utensils before starting to make sure that you have everything. Measure all the ingredients carefully. Put everything you need on a tray. When the tray is empty, you'll know you haven't left anything out!

- Reread the recipe to make sure that you haven't left anything out.

While You Cook

- Clean up as you cook—it makes less work at the end! After you finish using a utensil (except for sharp knives), put it in warm soapy water to soak. Wash sharp knives separately, and be careful of the sharp blades.

- Wash and dry all the utensils you have used, and put them away. Wash the counters, and leave the kitchen neat and clean.

- Check the range, oven and any other appliances to be sure that you have turned them off. Put away any appliances, such as a hand mixer, that you have used.

- Leaving the kitchen clean will make everyone glad to have you cook again. Now, enjoy your creation!

Playing It Safe in the Kitchen

Preparing the Food

- Before you use a sharp knife, can opener, blender, electric mixer, the range or oven, be sure someone older is in the kitchen to help you and to answer questions. Watch for additional **Adult help:** signs throughout the recipes.

- Always dry your hands after you wash them to avoid slippery fingers.

- Wipe up any spills right away to avoid slippery floors—then wash your hands again.

- When slicing or chopping ingredients, be sure to use a cutting board.

- Cut raw or cooked poultry, fish or meat on a hard, plastic cutting board.

- Always wash all utensils and hands immediately after handling raw poultry, fish or meat.

- Always turn the sharp edge of a knife or vegetable peeler away from you and your hand when you chop or peel foods.

- Turn off the electric mixer or blender before you scrape the sides of the bowl or container so that the scraper won't get caught in the blades.

- Turn off the electric mixer and be sure it's unplugged whenever you put the beaters in or take them out.

- To avoid burns, always use thick, dry pot holders, not thin or wet ones.

- Carefully remove casserole and pot lids by lifting the cover away from you to let the steam out. Keep your face away from the steam.

- Turn the handles of saucepans on the range away from you so that they don't catch on anything and tip over.

- Ask an adult to drain foods cooked in lots of hot water, like spaghetti. Pans full of hot water are heavy, and if it isn't done just right, the liquid and steam could burn you.

- Be careful where you put hot dishes. Only put them on a surface that is dry and can withstand heat.

Using Appliances

The Oven

- If the racks need to be adjusted higher or lower, be sure to move them before you turn on the oven.
- Allow plenty of air space around foods you're baking—no pans or dishes should touch.
- Arrange foods on oven racks so that one isn't placed directly over another.
- Use a tight-fitting lid or aluminum foil when the recipe calls for covering. Uncover cooked foods away from you, and keep your face away from the steam.
- Close the oven door quickly when you have finished looking in, so heat won't be lost.
- Ask an adult to help you put foods in and take foods out of the oven.

The Range or Stove Top

- Put large pans on large burners, small pans on small burners. Turn the handles of pots and pans so that they don't stick out over the edge of the range, where they might accidentally be bumped. Make sure that they do not cover another burner either.

The Microwave Oven

- Read the instruction booklet to find out the kinds of foods your oven cooks best and the correct cooking times.
- Most food should be covered to prevent spattering.
- Allow a few minutes' standing time after cooking foods because they continue to cook after you take them out of the oven.
- Be careful not to burn yourself. Even though microwaves go right through containers without heating them, the heat of the food can make the containers hot.

For the Cook's Adult Helper

Preparing food for themselves and others is very satisfying for children, and children love to cook! But precautions must be taught. Your supervision along with some simple rules can make it fun and, more importantly, safe for boys and girls to fix their own snacks and help prepare meals. You are the best judge of the age at which a child should be allowed to use the range, oven, other appliances or sharp knives. Follow these simple steps to help children cook safely:

- Read the recipe all the way through with the child before he or she starts to cook. Explain anything the child doesn't understand.

- We recommend adult supervision whenever children use raw meat, sharp knives, the range, the oven or small appliances.

- Teach children how to correctly set the controls on the range and oven.

- Provide pot holders in a size that's easy for smaller, less adept hands to use.

- Teach children safe food-preparation techniques and how to handle hot foods.

Table Talk

You can make mealtimes more fun by setting a nice-looking table. The photograph below shows you how to set the table correctly. If you like, put the napkin in a pretty napkin ring to make the table look really special!

Kitchen Computing

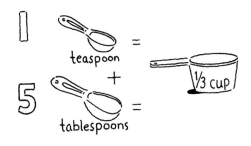

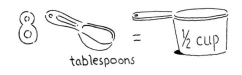

Making Good Food Choices

- To help you grow strong and feel good, you need to eat right. But what does it mean to "eat right"? Use the Food Guide Pyramid as your guide to plan your meals and snacks. It will help you eat right every day.

- The Food Guide Pyramid is divided into six parts, or food groups. The top section is Fats, Oils and Sweets, and most people need to limit their use of these foods. The 5 lower groups are all important, and you need food from all of them.

- Below the name of each food group are some numbers that tell you how many servings to eat from that group each day. You need more foods from the groups at the bottom, where it is wider, than you do from the top groups.

- At each meal, serve foods from at least 3 different food groups. Some foods, such as tacos, combine foods from 2 or more different groups. Do the best you can to estimate the servings from each food group.

- It's a good idea to plan for snacks just as you plan for meals. Keep a supply of healthy snack foods on hand, such as cut-up vegetables or low-fat crackers and cookies.

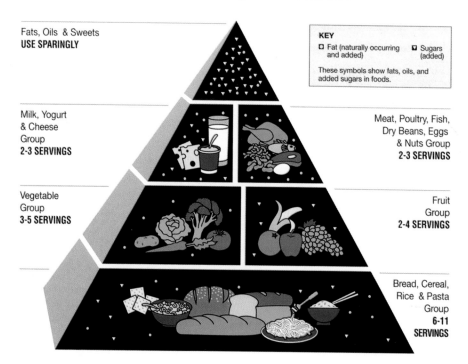

Food Guide Pyramid
A Guide to Daily Food Choices

Fats, Oils & Sweets
USE SPARINGLY

KEY
☐ Fat (naturally occurring and added)   ▌ Sugars (added)
These symbols show fats, oils, and added sugars in foods.

Milk, Yogurt & Cheese Group
2-3 SERVINGS

Meat, Poultry, Fish, Dry Beans, Eggs & Nuts Group
2-3 SERVINGS

Vegetable Group
3-5 SERVINGS

Fruit Group
2-4 SERVINGS

Bread, Cereal, Rice & Pasta Group
6-11 SERVINGS

Learning the Language

Beat: Make smooth with a vigorous stirring motion using a spoon, wire whisk, eggbeater or electric mixer.

Boil: Heat liquid until bubbles keep rising and breaking on the surface.

Chop: Cut food into small, uneven pieces; a sharp knife, food chopper or food processor can be used.

Core: Cut out the stem end and remove the seeds.

Cut in: Mix fat into a flour mixture with a pastry blender with a rolling motion or cut with a fork or two knives until particles are the size specified.

Dice: Cut into cubes smaller than 1/2 inch.

Drain: Pour off liquid or let it run off through the holes in a strainer or colander, as when draining cooked pasta or ground beef. Or, remove pieces of food from a fat or liquid and set them on paper towels to soak up excess moisture.

Flute: Flatten pastry evenly on rim of pie plate and press firmly around rim with tines of fork.

Grate: Rub against grater to cut into small pieces.

Grease: Spread the bottom and sides of a dish with butter or shortening using a pastry brush or paper towel.

Knead: Curve your fingers and fold dough toward you, then push it away with the heels of your hands, using a quick rocking motion.

Mix: Combine to distribute ingredients evenly using a spoon, fork, blender or an electric mixer.

Peel: Cut off the skin with a knife or peel with fingers.

Pipe: Press out frosting from a decorating bag using steady pressure to form a design or write a message. To finish a design, stop the pressure and lift the point up and away.

Roll or Pat: Flatten and spread with a floured rolling pin or hands.

Turn: To move the dish halfway around or 1/4 way around so that it cooks more evenly. Used in microwave for foods that can't be stirred.

Utensils You Should Have

For Preparation

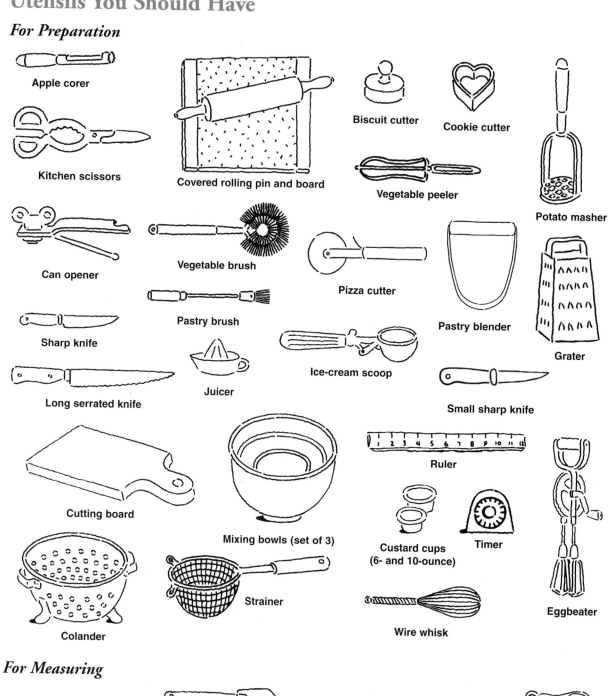

Apple corer

Kitchen scissors

Covered rolling pin and board

Biscuit cutter

Cookie cutter

Vegetable peeler

Potato masher

Can opener

Vegetable brush

Pizza cutter

Pastry blender

Pastry brush

Grater

Sharp knife

Ice-cream scoop

Long serrated knife

Juicer

Small sharp knife

Cutting board

Mixing bowls (set of 3)

Ruler

Custard cups
(6- and 10-ounce)

Timer

Colander

Strainer

Wire whisk

Eggbeater

For Measuring

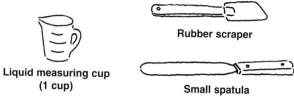

Liquid measuring cup
(1 cup)

Rubber scraper

Small spatula

Dry-ingredient measuring
cups (1-, 1/2-, 1/3-, 1/4-cup)

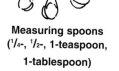

Measuring spoons
(1/4-, 1/2-, 1-teaspoon,
1-tablespoon)

For Top-of-Range Cooking

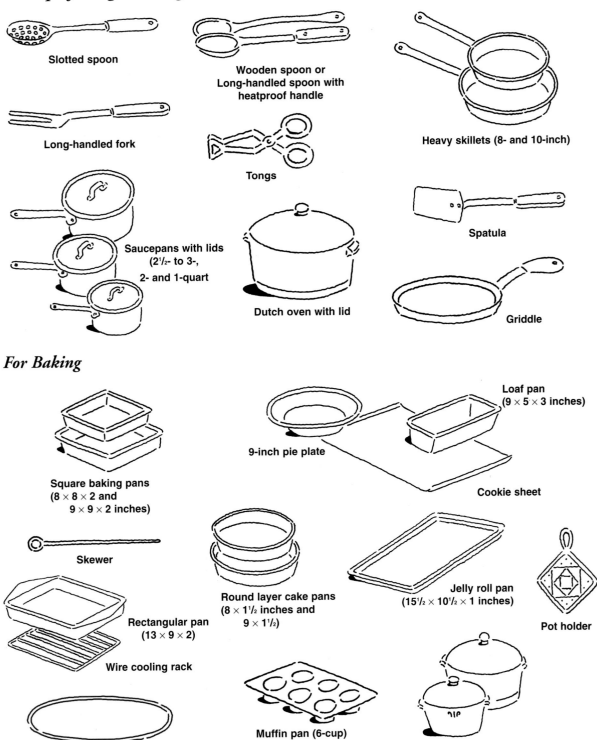

Slotted spoon

**Wooden spoon or
Long-handled spoon with
heatproof handle**

Heavy skillets (8- and 10-inch)

Long-handled fork

Tongs

**Saucepans with lids
(2½- to 3-,
2- and 1-quart**

Dutch oven with lid

Spatula

Griddle

For Baking

**Loaf pan
(9 × 5 × 3 inches)**

9-inch pie plate

Cookie sheet

**Square baking pans
(8 × 8 × 2 and
9 × 9 × 2 inches)**

Skewer

**Jelly roll pan
(15½ × 10½ × 1 inches)**

Pot holder

**Rectangular pan
(13 × 9 × 2)**

**Round layer cake pans
(8 × 1½ inches and
9 × 1½)**

Wire cooling rack

Pizza pan (14 inches)

Muffin pan (6-cup)

**Casseroles with lids
(1-, 2- or 3-quart)**

Measuring Up

 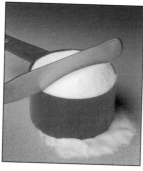

All-purpose Flour. Spoon flour lightly into dry-ingredient measuring cup. Level with spatula. Bisquick baking mix and granulated and powdered sugars are measured the same way.

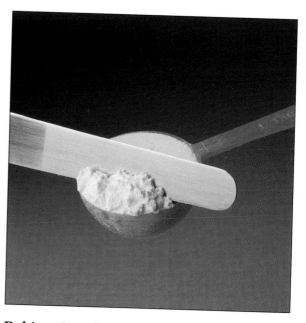

Baking Powder. Dip and fill measuring spoon. Level with spatula. Baking soda, cream of tartar and spices are measured in the same way. Liquids, like vanilla, can also be measured in measuring spoons.

Chopped Nuts. Pack lightly into dry-ingredient measuring cup. Also measure shredded cheese, soft bread crumbs and shredded coconut this way.

Brown Sugar. Pack firmly into dry-ingredient measuring cup. Level with spatula.

Shortening. Pack firmly into dry-ingredient measuring cup. Level with spatula and remove with rubber scraper.

Molasses and Corn Syrup. Pour into liquid measuring cup. Remove with rubber scraper.

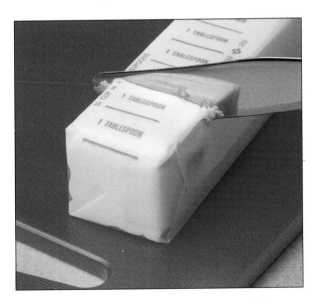

Margarine or Butter. Cut using measurement marks on the wrapper as a guide.

Milk and Other Liquids. Set liquid measuring cup on counter. Pour in the liquid. Bend down to check the correct amount at eye level.

1

▲▲▲▲▲▲▲▲

Breakfast Treats

Morning Muffin Meal (page 23)

SHAKE-'EM-UP
SCRAMBLED EGGS
4 servings

Utensils You Will Need

Sharp knife • Cutting board • 1-quart jar with lid • Dry-ingredient measuring cup • Measuring spoons • 10-inch skillet • Spatula

1 **Adult help:** Wash, then chop into 1/2-inch pieces and put in clean jar →

1 medium tomato

2 Add →

4 large eggs
1/2 cup shredded Cheddar cheese (2 ounces)
1/4 teaspoon salt
Dash of pepper

3 Cover the jar tightly and shake well.

4 Melt in skillet over medium heat, then tilt skillet so inside of skillet is coated with →

1 tablespoon margarine or butter

5 Pour egg mixture into skillet and cook without stirring. Turn eggs gently with spatula when the eggs in the bottom of the pan start to get firm. Cook 5 to 8 minutes or until eggs are slightly firm but not runny.

To Microwave:

Leave out margarine. Beat eggs, salt and pepper with fork in 1-quart microwavable casserole or bowl. Stir in the chopped tomato and cheese.

Cover casserole with lid or plastic wrap. If using plastic wrap, turn back 1 edge to make a little space for the steam to come out. Microwave on High (100%) 1 minute. Very carefully remove the lid, then stir.

Re-cover and microwave on High (100%) 3 minutes, stirring after each minute. (Dish may be hot at the end of cooking, so use pot holders.) Eggs should be slightly firm but not runny.

Here's another idea…Make **Green and Yellow Scrambled Eggs:** Use 1 small stalk celery, washed and chopped, or 1 small green bell pepper, washed and chopped, in place of the tomato. Add 1/4 cup milk.

Nutrition Per Serving: Calories 165 (Calories from Fat 115); Fat 13g (Saturated 5g); Cholesterol 230mg; Sodium 320mg; Carbohydrate 2g (Dietary Fiber 0g); Protein 10g

HINT
Always be sure to cook eggs until firm, not runny, to kill any bacteria.

▲▲▲▲▲ JELLY OMELET ▲▲▲▲▲

1 serving *(photo page 24)*

Utensils You Will Need

Small bowl • Fork • 8-inch skillet • Small sharp knife •
Measuring spoons • Plate

1 Beat in small bowl with fork - - - ▶

> **2 large eggs
> Dash of salt**

2 Melt in skillet or omelet pan over
medium-high heat, then tilt skillet
so the inside of skillet is coated with ▪ ▶

> **1 tablespoon margarine or butter**

3 Pour eggs into skillet. Tilt the skillet
to spread out the eggs. When edges
of the omelet become firm, pull the
edges gently toward the center with
a fork. Tilt the skillet to let the un-
cooked eggs run to the edge to cook.

4 When the omelet is set, spoon on top ▶

> **1 or 2 tablespoons jelly or jam
> (any flavor)**

5 **Adult help:** Loosen the edges of the
omelet with a fork or spatula. Hold the
handle of the skillet upward, fold
omelet over and roll it onto a plate.

To Microwave:

Follow step 1 above to beat eggs and salt. Put margarine in microwavable pie
plate, 9 × 1 1/4 inches. Put the pie plate on a microwavable dinner plate
turned upside down in the microwave. Microwave uncovered on High
(100%) 30 seconds or until margarine is melted. Tilt the pie plate so the
margarine covers the inside.

Pour beaten eggs into pie plate, then cover with waxed paper. (Put waxed paper on pie plate so it curls down instead of up. It will stay on better.)

Microwave on High (100%) 1 minute. Pull outer edge of omelet to center with fork and gently shake pie plate to spread eggs evenly. Re-cover and microwave on High (100%) 1 to 1 1/2 minutes longer or until center is set but still moist. Finish recipe starting at step 5 above.

Nutrition Per Serving: Calories 295 (Calories from Fat 190); Fat 21g (Saturated 5g); Cholesterol 430mg; Sodium 530mg; Carbohydrate 13g (Dietary Fiber 0g); Protein 13g

◢◣◢◣◢◣ MORNING MUFFIN MEAL ◢◣◢◣◢◣

4 servings

🍴🥄🔪 Utensils You Will Need

Fork • Toaster • Spatula • Measuring cup

1 Split with fork, then toast ━ ━ ━ ➤ **4 English muffins**

2 Cook as directed on package ━ ━ ━ ➤ **4 sausage patties**

3 Cook Shake-'em-up Scrambled Eggs (page 20), leaving out the tomatoes and cheese.

4 To assemble each muffin, top 1 half of muffin with about 1/4 cup scrambled eggs. Put 1 sausage patty on top of eggs. Top with other half of muffin.

Here's another idea…Make **Bacon or Ham Muffin Meal:** Use cooked bacon or ham in place of the sausage.

Nutrition Per Serving: Calories 335 (Calories from Fat 170); Fat 19g (Saturated 6g); Cholesterol 230mg; Sodium 710mg; Carbohydrate 28g (Dietary Fiber 1g); Protein 14g

▲▲▲▲▲ EGG IN A FRAME ▲▲▲▲▲

1 serving

🍴 Utensils You Will Need

2 1/2-inch Biscuit cutter • Knife • 8-inch skillet with lid • Spatula

1 Cut out center with biscuit cutter or tear a 2 1/2-inch circle from - - - ▶ | **1 slice bread** |

2 Spread generously on both sides of bread - - - - - - ▶ | **Margarine or butter, softened** |

3 Put bread "frame" in 8-inch skillet. Cook over medium heat 4 to 5 minutes or until bread is golden brown on the bottom. Turn bread over, using spatula.

4 Break into measuring cup or saucer, then carefully slip into circle - - - ▶ | **1 large egg** |

5 Turn heat down to low. Cover skillet and cook 5 to 7 minutes or until egg is firm.

6 Sprinkle lightly with - - - - - ▶ | **Salt** |

7 Lift egg and bread from skillet, using spatula.

Nutrition Per Serving: Calories 190 (Calories from Fat 110); Fat 12g (Saturated 3g); Cholesterol 210mg; Sodium 400mg; Carbohydrate 13g (Dietary Fiber 0g); Protein 8g

Jelly Omelet (page 22)

▲▲▲▲▲ BIG PUFFY PANCAKE ▲▲▲▲▲

4 servings

🍴 Utensils You Will Need

Pie plate, 10 × 1 1/2 inches • Pot holders • Medium bowl • Eggbeater •
Dry-ingredient measuring cup • Liquid measuring cup • Measuring spoons •
Rubber scraper • Sharp knife • Spatula

1 Heat oven to 425°.

2 Put in pie plate - - - - - - - ➤ | **3 tablespoons margarine or butter**

3 **Adult help:** Heat in oven just until margarine is melted.

4 Beat in medium bowl with eggbeater until smooth - - - ➤ | **1/2 cup all-purpose flour** / **1/2 cup milk** / **1/8 teaspoon salt** / **4 large eggs**

5 Stir in the melted margarine.

6 Gently stir in with rubber scraper - - ➤ | **1/2 cup fresh or frozen (thawed and drained) blueberries**

7 Pour batter into pie plate.

8 **Adult help:** Bake about 25 minutes or until pancake is puffy and golden brown. Carefully remove from oven.

9 If you like, fill pancake with - - - ➤ | **Fresh fruit**

10 Sprinkle with - - - - - - - ➤ | **Powdered sugar**

11 Cut pancake into 4 wedges and serve with maple-flavored syrup, if you like.

Nutrition Per Serving: Calories 225 (Calories from Fat 125); Fat 14g (Saturated 4g); Cholesterol 210mg; Sodium 250mg; Carbohydrate 17g (Dietary Fiber 1g); Protein 9g

▲▲▲▲▲ FAVORITE FRENCH TOAST ▲▲▲▲

6 servings

🍴 Utensils You Will Need

Griddle • Pastry brush • Small bowl • Fork • Liquid measuring cup •
Measuring spoons • Spatula

1 Heat griddle over medium heat, or heat electric skillet to 375°. (To test griddle or skillet, sprinkle with a few drops of water. If bubbles jump around, heat is just right.)

2 Grease griddle with ▪ ▪ ▪ ▪ ▶ | **Margarine** |

3 Mix in small bowl with fork ▪ ▪ ▪ ▶ | **2 large eggs**
1/2 cup milk
1/4 teaspoon salt |

4 Dip in egg mixture ▪ ▪ ▪ ▪ ▪ ▶ | **6 slices day-old bread** |

5 Cook bread on griddle about 4 minutes or until bottoms are golden brown (lift an edge and peek). Turn bread with spatula. Cook other sides about 4 minutes or until bottoms are golden brown.

6 Serve with ▪ ▪ ▪ ▪ ▪ ▪ ▶ | **Powdered sugar or your favorite syrup** |

Nutrition Per Serving: Calories 115 (Calories from Fat 35); Fat 4g (Saturated 1g); Cholesterol 75mg; Sodium 250mg; Carbohydrate 15g (Dietary Fiber 0g); Protein 5g

WHOLE WHEAT WAFFLES

Three 10-inch waffles

Utensils You Will Need

Waffle iron • Large bowl • Dry-ingredient measuring cup • Liquid measuring cup • Measuring spoons • Eggbeater • Pastry brush • Fork

1 Heat waffle iron.

2 Beat in large bowl with eggbeater until fluffy - - - - - ▶

| 2 large eggs |

3 Beat in just until smooth - - - - ▶

| 2 cups whole wheat flour |
| 1 3/4 cups milk |
| 1/2 cup (1 stick) margarine or butter, melted, or vegetable oil |
| 1 tablespoon packed brown sugar |
| 4 teaspoons baking powder |
| 1/2 teaspoon salt |

4 Grease waffle iron with - - - - ▶

| Margarine |

5 For each waffle, pour batter from cup or pitcher onto center of hot waffle iron. Bake about 5 minutes or until steaming stops. Carefully remove waffle with fork.

Nutrition Per Waffle Square: Calories 675 (Calories from Fat 340); Fat 38g (Saturated 9g); Cholesterol 150mg; Sodium 1480mg; Carbohydrate 72g (Dietary Fiber 9g); Protein 20g

Adam had fun pouring the batter into the waffle iron. And according to his mom, the waffles are "sister approved."

MOTHER'S DAY BREAKFAST IN BED

What a terrific treat for Mom on her special day! Making breakfast for Mom to enjoy in bed is a great project for siblings—or for kids and dads. We suggest serving fresh berries because they don't need to be peeled or cut up, but any fresh fruit would be fine. Follow the Easy Plan below, add some fresh flowers and don't forget to clean up the kitchen for a Mother's Day morning that says to Mom, I love you!

Menu

Shake-'em-up Scrambled Eggs page 20

Crumb-topped Breakfast Cake page 38

Mixed Fresh Berries

Homemade Hot Cocoa Mix page 74

Tropical Fruit Juice Blend

Easy Breakfast Plan

1 Several days before Mother's Day, make up a shopping list from the menu and recipes and buy the ingredients that you need. Mix up the Homemade Hot Cocoa Mix.

2 The evening before, set the tray and gather all the equipment you will need. Mix up the dry ingredients in step 3 of Crumb-topped Breakfast Cake. Cover bowl and leave at room temperature overnight.

3 First thing Mother's Day morning, finish making the breakfast cake. While the cake is baking, get everything ready for the Shake-'em-up Scrambled Eggs.

4 When the cake comes out of the oven, cook the eggs and heat the milk for the cocoa. Pour the juice, make the cocoa and arrange everything on the tray.

Shake-'em-up Scrambled Eggs, Crumb-topped Breakfast Cake, Homemade Hot Cocoa Mix

▲▲▲▲▲ OATMEAL PANCAKES ▲▲▲▲▲

10 pancakes

Utensils You Will Need

Medium bowl • Dry-ingredient measuring cups • Liquid measuring cup • Measuring spoons • Eggbeater • Griddle • Pot holders • Spatula

1 Beat in medium bowl with eggbeater until smooth (for thinner pancakes, stir in 2 to 4 tablespoons more milk) ▪➤

1/2 cup all-purpose flour
1/2 cup quick-cooking oats
3/4 cup buttermilk
1/4 cup milk
1 tablespoon sugar
2 tablespoons vegetable oil
1 teaspoon baking powder
1/2 teaspoon baking soda
1/2 teaspoon salt
1 large egg

2 **Adult help:** Heat griddle over medium heat, or heat electric skillet to 375°. (To test griddle or skillet, sprinkle with a few drops of water. If bubbles jump around, heat is just right.)

3 If needed, grease griddle or electric skillet with – – – – – – – ➤

Margarine

4 For each pancake, pour a little less than 1/4 cup batter onto hot griddle. Cook until pancakes are puffed and dry around edges. Turn pancakes. Cook other sides of pancakes until golden brown. Serve pancakes with Peanut Butter Spread (page 34).

Nutrition Per Serving: Calories 90 (Calories from Fat 35); Fat 4g (Saturated 1g); Cholesterol 25mg; Sodium 250mg; Carbohydrate 10g (Dietary Fiber 0g); Protein 3g

According to Shawyn, "It looked like mud and was fun to play with in the bowl, and I made shapes in the skillet with the batter." We give Shawyn an A+ for creativity!

HOMEMADE PANCAKE
▲▲▲▲▲ SYRUP ▲▲▲▲▲

1 3/4 cups syrup

 **Utensils You Will Need**

l-quart saucepan • Dry-ingredient measuring cups • Liquid measuring cup •
Small sharp knife • Measuring spoons • Wooden spoon

1 Mix in saucepan with wooden spoon ▪►

> **1 1/2 cups packed brown sugar**
> **3/4 cup water**
> **1 tablespoon margarine or butter**
> **Dash of salt**

2 Heat to boiling over medium heat,
stirring all the time. Remove saucepan
from heat.

3 Stir in - - - - - - - - - - - - ►

> **1/2 teaspoon maple flavoring**

4 Serve warm.

To Microwave:

Use 1/2 cup water in place of the 3/4 cup water. Stir brown sugar, water,
margarine and salt in 4-cup microwavable measuring cup. Microwave
uncovered on High (100%) 2 minutes, then stir.

Microwave on High (100%) 1 to 1 1/2 minutes longer or until boiling. Stir
in maple flavoring. Stir before serving.

*Nutrition Per 2 Tablespoons: Calories 50 (Calories from Fat 0); Fat 0g (Saturated 0g); Cholesterol 0mg;
Sodium 20mg; Carbohydrate 12g (Dietary Fiber 0g); Protein 0g*

PEANUT BUTTER
▲▲▲▲▲ SPREAD ▲▲▲▲▲

1 cup spread

🍴 Utensils You Will Need

Small bowl • Dry-ingredient measuring cup • Liquid measuring cup • Fork

1 Mix in small bowl with fork ▬ ▬ ▬ ➤

1/2 cup peanut butter
1/2 cup maple-flavored syrup

2 Cover leftover spread and store at room
temperature.

Nutrition Per Tablespoon: Calories 80 (Calories from Fat 35); Fat 4g (Saturated 1g); Cholesterol 0mg; Sodium 50mg; Carbohydrate 9g (Dietary Fiber 0g); Protein 2g

**Shawyn thinks this easy and good spread he
can make himself would be great as an
after-school snack.**

▲▲▲▲▲ HONEY BUTTER ▲▲▲▲▲

1 cup spread

 **Utensils You Will Need**

Small bowl • Liquid measuring cup • Fork

1 Mix in small bowl with fork ▬ ▬ ▬ ▬ ➤

> 1/2 cup (1 stick) margarine or
> butter, softened
> 1/2 cup honey

2 Cover leftover spread and store in refrigerator. Let spread warm to room temperature before using.

Nutrition Per Tablespoon: Calories 90 (Calories from Fat 55); Fat 6g (Saturated 1g); Cholesterol 0mg; Sodium 70mg; Carbohydrate 9g (Dietary Fiber 0g); Protein 0g

This recipe is easy to make, and Adam says his whole family likes it a lot. His mom suggests cutting the amounts in half if you don't want to have leftovers on hand.

LEMON-BLUEBERRY MUFFINS

12 muffins

Utensils You Will Need

Muffin pan with medium cups, 2 1/2 × 1 1/4 inches • Pastry brush •
Fork • Medium bowl • Wooden spoon • Dry-ingredient measuring cups •
Measuring spoons • Pot holders

1 Heat oven to 400°.

2 Line 12 muffin cups with paper baking cups or grease bottoms only with ▬ ▬ ▬ ▬ ▬ ▬ ▶ | **Shortening** |

3 Beat slightly in medium bowl with fork ▬ ▬ ▬ ▬ ▬ ▶ | **1 large egg** |

4 Stir in just until all the baking mix is wet (do not stir too much; batter will be thick) ▬ ▬ ▬ ▬ ▬ ▶

> **2 cups Bisquick Original baking mix**
> **1/4 cup sugar**
> **2 tablespoons vegetable oil**
> **1 container (6 ounces) lemon yogurt**

5 Gently stir in ▬ ▬ ▬ ▬ ▬ ▶

> **3/4 cup fresh or frozen (thawed and drained) blueberries**

6 Spoon batter into muffin cups until 2/3 full.

7 Bake 15 to 18 minutes or until golden brown. Immediately remove muffins from pan to wire rack. Serve warm or cool.

Nutrition Per Muffin: Calories 140 (Calories from Fat 55); Fat 6g (Saturated 1g); Cholesterol 20mg; Sodium 300mg; Carbohydrate 20g (Dietary Fiber 0g); Protein 2g

Lemon-Blueberry Muffins

CRUMB-TOPPED
▲▲▲▲▲ BREAKFAST CAKE ▲▲▲▲▲
9 servings

Utensils You Will Need

Square pan, 9×9×2 inches • Pastry brush • Large bowl • Dry-ingredient measuring cups • Measuring spoons • Wooden spoons • Small sharp knife • Pastry blender • Liquid measuring cup • Fork • Pot holders • Toothpick • Wire cooling rack • Small bowl • Spoon

1 Heat oven to 375°.

2 Grease square pan with - - - - - ▶   **Shortening**

3 Mix in large bowl with wooden spoon - - - - - - - - - - ▶

> **2 1/4 cups all-purpose flour**
> **1 1/4 cups sugar**
> **1 teaspoon salt**
> **1 teaspoon baking soda**
> **1 teaspoon ground cinnamon**
> **1 teaspoon ground nutmeg**
> **1/2 teaspoon ground cloves**
> **1/2 teaspoon ground allspice**

4 Cut into flour mixture with pastry blender until mixture looks like small crumbs - - - - - - - ▶

> **3/4 cup (1 1/2 sticks) firm margarine or butter**

5 Save 1 cup of crumb mixture.

6 Stir into rest of crumb mixture just until flour is wet (batter will be thick and lumpy) - - - - - - ▶

> **1 cup chopped walnuts**
> **1 cup buttermilk**
> **1 large egg, slightly beaten**

7 Pour batter into pan. Sprinkle saved crumb mixture over batter.

8 Bake 40 to 45 minutes or until toothpick poked in center comes out clean. Put pan on wire rack.

9 Mix in small bowl with spoon, adding water 1 teaspoon at a time, until thin enough to drizzle - - - →

> **1 cup powdered sugar**
> **2 tablespoons margarine or butter, melted**
> **1/2 teaspoon vanilla**
> **3 to 4 teaspoons hot water**

10 Drizzle glaze over warm coffee cake. Serve warm.

Nutrition Per Serving: Calories 540 (Calories from Fat 245); Fat 27g (Saturated 5g); Cholesterol 25mg; Sodium 620mg; Carbohydrate 69g (Dietary Fiber 2g); Protein 7g

The crumbs on top of this breakfast cake were Katie's favorite and she said, "It tastes good on a Saturday morning."

GRANOLA-CINNAMON ▲▲▲▲▲ TOAST ▲▲▲▲▲

1 cup spread

🍴 Utensils You Will Need

Small bowl • Dry-ingredient measuring cups • Measuring spoons •
Wooden spoon • Knife

1 Mix in small bowl with wooden spoon ▸

> **3/4 cup granola (any flavor)**
> **1/2 cup peanut butter**
> **1/2 teaspoon ground cinnamon**

2 Spread 2 tablespoons on ▸

> **Each slice of toast**

3 This makes enough for 8 slices of toast.
Cover leftover spread and store at room temperature.

Here's another idea…Make **Granola Cinnamon Toast for a Crowd:** Set oven control to broil. Make Granola-Cinnamon Toast, spreading 2 tablespoons of granola mix on each of 8 slices bread. Put bread on broiler pan. **Adult help:** Broil bread with tops 3 inches from heat about 2 minutes or until spread is bubbly and light brown. Remove bread from broiler pan with spatula.

Nutrition Per Piece of Toast: Calories 210 (Calories from Fat 100); Fat 11g (Saturated 3g); Cholesterol 0mg; Sodium 220mg; Carbohydrate 22g (Dietary Fiber 2g); Protein 7g

Jamie will definitely make this recipe again to have on hand. She says, "It's breakfast in 2 minutes!"

Stuffed Apple Halves (page 42)

▲▲▲▲ STUFFED APPLE HALVES ▲▲▲▲

4 servings *(photo page 41)*

🍴 Utensils You Will Need

Small sharp knife • Melon baller • Small bowl • Measuring spoons • Spoon • 10-inch skillet • Liquid measuring cup • Pot holders • Fork

1 Adult help: Cut in half with knife, and then remove cores, using melon baller or grapefruit spoon, from ‐ ‐ ‐ ➤

> **2 medium red cooking apples**

2 Mix in small bowl with spoon ‐ ‐ ‐ ‐ ➤

> **2 tablespoons raisins, finely chopped**
> **2 tablespoons walnuts, finely chopped**
> **1 tablespoon packed brown sugar**
> **1 tablespoon margarine or butter**

3 Press raisin mixture into centers of apple halves.

4 Put in skillet ‐ ‐ ‐ ‐ ‐ ‐ ‐ ➤

> **1 cup apple juice or cider**
> **3 whole cloves**

5 Put apple halves in skillet with stuffed sides up.

6 Heat mixture in skillet until apple juice is boiling. Turn heat down to low. Cover and simmer about 15 minutes or until apples are tender when poked with fork. Remove apple halves from skillet with slotted spoon. Remove cloves from juice, and spoon juice over apples.

To Microwave:

Follow steps 1 through 5 above—except put apples in microwavable 2-quart casserole instead of skillet. Cover casserole with lid or plastic wrap. If using plastic wrap, turn back 1 edge to make a little space for the steam to come out.

Microwave on High (100%) 2 minutes. Turn casserole 1/2 turn. Microwave on High (100%) 1 to 3 minutes longer or until apples are tender when poked with a fork. (Dish may be hot at the end of cooking, so use pot holders.)

Nutrition Per Serving: Calories 155 (Calories from Fat 55); Fat 6g (Saturated 1g); Cholesterol 0mg; Sodium 35mg; Carbohydrate 27g (Dietary Fiber 2g); Protein 1g

Jared had cranberry-flavored apple juice on hand, so he used that instead of the apple juice. Both Jared and his two younger brothers enjoyed eating the apples!

ORANGE-GLAZED ▲▲▲▲▲ BANANAS ▲▲▲▲▲

4 servings

Utensils You Will Need

1-quart casserole • Small sharp knife • Dry-ingredient measuring cup •
Liquid measuring cup • Wooden spoon • Measuring spoons • Pot holders

1 Heat oven to 375°.

2 Adult help: Slice with small sharp knife ----→

> **2 bananas**

3 Mix in casserole with wooden spoon ----→

> **2 bananas, sliced**
> **1/4 cup raisins**
> **1/3 cup orange juice**

4 Sprinkle banana mixture with --→

> **2 tablespoons flaked coconut**

5 Bake uncovered about 10 minutes or until coconut is golden brown.
Serve warm.

To Microwave:

Follow steps 2 and 3 above, using a 1-quart microwavable casserole. Cover casserole with lid or plastic wrap. If using plastic wrap, turn back 1 edge to make a little space for the steam to come out.

Microwave on High (100%) 1 minute. Very carefully remove the lid, then stir. Re-cover and microwave on High (100%) 30 seconds to 1 minute or until bananas are hot. (Dish may be hot at the end of cooking, so use pot holders.)

Nutrition Per Serving: Calories 109 (Calories from Fat 10); Fat 1g (Saturated 1g); Cholesterol 0mg; Sodium 10mg; Carbohydrate 25g (Dietary Fiber 1g); Protein 1g

Leslie had a decorating idea for this morning fruit dish. "After I baked it, I took a fork and made a design in the dish so the bananas and raisins alternated around the dish."

2

▲▲▲▲▲▲▲

Super-Duper Snacks and Drinks

Frosty Fruity Sodas (page 71), Very Beary Snack Mix (page 55)

▲▲▲▲▲ PIZZA CORN SNACKS ▲▲▲▲▲

4 servings

Utensils You Will Need

Small sharp knife • 1-quart saucepan • Large bowl • Wooden spoon •
Dry-ingredient measuring cups • 12-inch pizza pan • Pot holders • Small bowls

1 Heat oven to 300°.

2 Adult help: Melt in saucepan over
low heat – – – – – – – – ➤ | **1/3 cup margarine or butter**

3 Toss in large bowl with wooden spoon
until well coated – – – – – – ➤ | **The melted margarine**
5 cups horn-shaped corn snacks

4 Toss snack mixture with – – – – ➤ | **1/3 cup grated Parmesan cheese**

5 Spread snack mixture on pizza pan or
heatproof serving plate. Bake 5 minutes. Pour snack mixture into small bowl.

6 Pour into second small bowl and
dip snacks into – – – – – – – ➤ | **1 can (8 ounces) pizza sauce**

*Nutrition Per Serving: Calories 430 (Calories from Fat 305); Fat 34g (Saturated 17g);
Cholesterol 5mg; Sodium 1040mg; Carbohydrate 27g (Dietary Fiber 2g); Protein 6g*

**Katie says, "They were fun to make and fun to
eat." She especially likes the taste of the corn
snacks in this savory treat.**

PINEAPPLE-CHEESE BALLS

About 34 snacks

 **Utensils You Will Need**

Cookie sheet • Waxed paper • Plastic bag with zipper top • Rolling pin •
Small bowl • Medium bowl • Can opener • Wooden spoon • Teaspoon •
Dry-ingredient measuring cup

1 Line cookie sheet with waxed paper.

2 Put in plastic bag - - - - - - - - ➤ | **1 1/2 cups granola**

3 Press air out of plastic bag, then seal.
Roll granola with rolling pin or jar until finely crushed.
Pour granola into small bowl.

4 Mix in medium bowl with wooden
spoon - - - - - - - - - ➤ | **1 package (8 ounces) cream cheese, softened**
1 can (8.25 ounces) crushed pineapple in syrup, well drained

5 Drop cream cheese mixture by
slightly rounded teaspoonfuls into
crushed granola. Roll cream cheese
mixture around in granola until coated. Shape into balls.

6 Put balls on waxed paper on cookie sheet. Refrigerate at least 1 hour. Cover
leftover balls and store in refrigerator.

Nutrition Per Snack: Calories 45 (Calories from Fat 25); Fat 3g (Saturated 2g);
Cholesterol 10mg; Sodium 20mg; Carbohydrate 3g (Dietary Fiber 0g); Protein 1g

**Jenna enjoyed rolling these tasty treats and
suggests adding a half cup of granola to the
cheese mixture if it's too sticky to work with.
That's a good tip, Jenna.**

▲▲▲▲ NIFTY NACHOS ▲▲▲▲

5 servings

🍴🥄🔪 Utensils You Will Need

Cookie sheet • Aluminum foil • Can opener • Dry-ingredient measuring cups • Pot holders

1 Heat oven to 400°. Line cookie sheet with aluminum foil.

2 Put on cookie sheet - - - - - - → | **30 tortilla chips** |

3 Sprinkle evenly over tortilla chips - → | **1/4 cup salsa or canned chopped mild green chilies, drained** |

4 Sprinkle on top of the salsa and chips - - - - - - - - → | **1 1/4 cups shredded Monterey Jack or Cheddar cheese (5 ounces)** |

5 Bake about 4 minutes or until cheese is melted.

To Microwave 1 serving:

Put 6 tortilla chips in a circle on microwavable dinner plate. Spoon a small amount of salsa on each chip. Sprinkle with shredded cheese. Microwave uncovered on High (100%) 20 to 30 seconds or until cheese is melted.

Nutrition Per Serving: Calories 180 (Calories from Fat 115); Fat 13g (Saturated 6g); Cholesterol 30mg; Sodium 350mg; Carbohydrate 9g (Dietary Fiber 0g); Protein 7g

▲▲▲▲▲ BUMPY CELERY STICKS ▲▲▲▲▲

6 snacks

Utensils You Will Need

10-inch skillet • Small sharp knife • Dry-ingredient measuring cup •
Measuring spoons • Wooden spoons • Small bowl • Knife

1 Adult help: Melt in skillet over low heat - - - - - - ►
> **1 tablespoon margarine or butter**

2 Remove skillet from heat and stir in ■ ►
> **1 cup crispy corn puff cereal**
> **1/4 teaspoon garlic salt**

3 Mix in small bowl with wooden spoon until smooth and creamy ■ ■ ►
> **1 package (3 ounces) cream cheese, softened**
> **1 tablespoon chili sauce**
> **1 teaspoon Worcestershire sauce**

4 Fill with cream cheese mixture ■ ■ ►
> **6 three-inch pieces celery (2 to 3 stalks)**

5 Sprinkle cereal over cream cheese mixture and press gently. Serve right away.

Nutrition Per Snack: Calories 85 (Calories from Fat 65); Fat 7g (Saturated 4g); Cholesterol 15mg; Sodium 190mg; Carbohydrate 5g (Dietary Fiber 0g); Protein 1g

Melting the margarine on the stove top was fun in this super easy recipe, according to Rachel. She suggests making these with process cheese spread in place of the cream cheese. We agree it makes a tasty variation!

HINT
*To soften cream cheese,
microwave unwrapped cheese
in small microwavable
dish on Medium (50%)
30 to 45 seconds.*

▲▲▲▲▲ SNICKERSNACK ▲▲▲▲▲

7 cups snack

Utensils You Will Need

Large bowl • Dry-ingredient measuring cup • Wooden spoon • 1-quart saucepan • Small sharp knife • Fork • Plastic bag

1 Mix in large bowl with wooden spoon ━ ━ ━ ━ ━ ━ ━ ━ ▶

> **4 cups toasted whole-grain oat cereal**
> **1 cup raisins**
> **1 cup salted peanuts**

2 **Adult help:** Melt in saucepan over low heat ━ ━ ━ ━ ━ ━ ━ ▶

> **1/4 cup (1/2 stick) margarine or butter**

3 Pour the melted margarine over the cereal mixture, using fork to toss lightly until the mixture is coated.

4 Sprinkle over cereal mixture, then toss again ━ ━ ━ ━ ━ ━ ━ ▶

> **1 package (6 ounces) semisweet chocolate chips (1 cup)**

5 Store snack in a sealed plastic bag or covered container.

Nutrition Per 1/2 Cup: Calories 225 (Calories from Fat 125); Fat 14g (Saturated 4g); Cholesterol 0mg; Sodium 160mg; Carbohydrate 23g (Dietary Fiber 3g); Protein 5g

▲▲▲▲▲ VERY BEARY SNACK MIX ▲▲▲▲▲

6 cups snack

Utensils You Will Need

Large bowl • Dry-ingredient measuring cups • Wooden spoon

1 Mix in large bowl with wooden spoon - - - - - - - - →

2 Store snack mix in a sealed plastic bag or airtight container at room temperature up to 5 days.

> 3 cups teddy bear-shaped graham snacks (any flavor)
> 1 cup dry-roasted peanuts
> 1 cup raisins
> 3 pouches (half of 5.4-ounce package) chewy fruit snack in bear shapes (any flavor)

Nutrition Per 1/2 Cup: Calories 145 (Calories from Fat 45); Fat 5g (Saturated 1g); Cholesterol 0mg; Sodium 95mg; Carbohydrate 24g (Dietary Fiber 2g); Protein 3g

Jenna's thoughts after trying this quick snack mix? "It's easy and very good to eat. It's a healthy snack."

▲▲▲▲FRUIT IN A CONE▲▲▲▲

1 cone

Utensils You Will Need

Dry-ingredient measuring cup • Sharp knife • Cutting board •
Measuring spoons

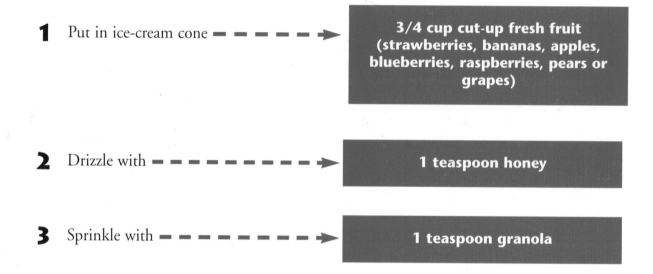

1 Put in ice-cream cone ➤ **3/4 cup cut-up fresh fruit (strawberries, bananas, apples, blueberries, raspberries, pears or grapes)**

2 Drizzle with ➤ **1 teaspoon honey**

3 Sprinkle with ➤ **1 teaspoon granola**

Nutrition Per Cone: Calories 80 (Calories from Fat 10); Fat 1g (Saturated 0g); Cholesterol 0mg; Sodium 10mg; Carbohydrate 19g (Dietary Fiber 2g); Protein 1g

STRAWBERRY FRUIT ▲▲▲▲▲ LEATHER ▲▲▲▲▲

1 roll

▲▲▲ Utensils You Will Need

Jelly roll pan, 15 1/2 × 10 1/2 × 1 inch • Plastic wrap • Blender • Sharp knife • Cutting board • Dry-ingredient measuring cup • Measuring spoons • Rubber scraper • Pot holders

1 Heat oven to 140° or Low. Line jelly roll pan with plastic wrap.

2 Put in blender ━ ━ ━ ━ ━ ➤

> **1 cup cut-up strawberries**
> **2 teaspoons honey or corn syrup**

3 Cover blender. Blend on high speed about 10 seconds or until strawberry mixture is smooth.

4 Pour strawberry mixture into center of jelly roll pan. Spread mixture evenly in the pan with rubber scraper.

5 Bake with oven door slightly open about 3 hours or until dry. Cool in pan. Roll in plastic wrap to store.

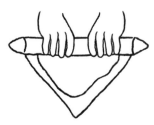

Nutrition Per Roll: Calories 95 (Calories from Fat 10); Fat 1g (Saturated 0g); Cholesterol 0mg; Sodium 5mg; Carbohydrate 23g (Dietary Fiber 2g); Protein 1g

▲▲▲▲▲ EASY CHEESY SPREAD ▲▲▲▲▲

1 1/3 cups spread

Utensils You Will Need

Medium bowl • Dry-ingredient measuring cup • Measuring spoons •
Wooden spoon • Small bowl • Plastic wrap

1 Mix in medium bowl with wooden
spoon - - - - - - - - - - - - →

> **1 container (8 ounces) whipped
> cream cheese
> 1 cup finely shredded Cheddar
> cheese (4 ounces)
> 1 teaspoon Dijon or regular
> prepared mustard
> 1 teaspoon Worcestershire sauce
> 1/2 teaspoon instant minced
> onion**

2 Put cheese mixture in small bowl.

3 Sprinkle with - - - - - - - - → **2 tablespoons chopped nuts**

4 Cover with plastic wrap and
refrigerate about 2 hours or until cold. Serve spread with crackers.

Here's another idea… Make a **Fuzzy Cheese Ball:** Do not sprinkle
Easy Cheesy Spread with nuts. After refrigerating for 2 hours, shape
the cheese mixture into a ball on waxed paper.
Roll cheese ball in 1/4 cup finely shredded
Cheddar cheese. Use olives for eyes and tortilla chips
for ears to make a face, if you like.

HINT
*Easy Cheesy Spread
is also good for
sandwiches.*

*Nutrition Per Tablespoon: Calories 65 (Calories from Fat 55); Fat 6g
(Saturated 4g); Cholesterol 20mg; Sodium 70mg; Carbohydrate 1g
(Dietary Fiber 0g); Protein 2g*

AFTER-THE-GAME CELEBRATION

Whether you win or lose, a tasty treat is always welcome after an exciting game. These recipes can easily be carted to the ballpark or can be awaiting the arrival of the team at home. Don't forget paper plates and napkins. Divide up the recipes and have a different team member make each recipe or make them yourself. Either way, follow the Easy Plan for a wholesome, satisfying celebration sure to please any future All-American.

Menu

Snickersnack   page 54

Zippy Vegetable Dip   page 64

Homemade Granola Bars   page 66

Oh-So-Chocolate Brownies   page 154

Boxes or Cans of Juice

Easy Game Plan

1 Several days before the game, make up a shopping list from the menu and recipes and buy the ingredients that you need.

2 Two days before, make the Snickersnack.

3 The day before, make the Homemade Granola Bars and Oh-So-Chocolate Brownies.

4 The morning of the game, make the Zippy Vegetable Dip and cut up the vegetables. Cover the dip and seal the vegetables in a plastic bag and store in the refrigerator.

5 If taking the celebration to the park, pack the dip, vegetables and juices with ice in a cooler.

Snickersnack, Zippy Vegetable Dip, Homemade Granola Bars, Oh-So-Chocolate Brownies

▲▲▲▲▲ QUICK FRUIT DIP ▲▲▲▲▲

1 cup dip

🍴 Utensils You Will Need

Small bowl • Dry-ingredient measuring cup • Measuring spoons •
Spoon • Sharp knife • Cutting board

1 Mix in small bowl with spoon ▬ ▬ ▬ ➤

> **1 cup plain yogurt**
> **2 tablespoons packed brown sugar**

2 Put dip in serving bowl. Serve with any of these fruit "dippers" ▬ ▬ ▬ ➤

> **Apple wedges**
> **Strawberries**
> **Grapes**
> **Banana slices**
> **Pineapple chunks**
> **Your favorite fresh fruit**

Nutrition Per Tablespoon: Calories 35 (Calories from Fat 10); Fat 1g (Saturated 0g); Cholesterol 5mg; Sodium 25mg; Carbohydrate 6g (Dietary Fiber 0g); Protein 1g

Quick Fruit Dip, Very Strawberry Soda (page 72)

▲▲▲▲ ZIPPY VEGETABLE DIP ▲▲▲▲

2 cups dip

Utensils You Will Need

Blender • Dry-ingredient measuring cup • Kitchen scissors • Rubber scraper • Serving bowl • Sharp knife • Cutting board

1 Put in blender - - - - - - - ➤

> **1 cup cottage cheese**
> **1 cup plain yogurt or sour cream**
> **1 envelope (1 ounce) ranch-style salad dressing mix**

2 Cover blender. Blend on medium speed about 30 seconds or until mixture is smooth. Stop the blender a few times to scrape mixture down from the sides. (Be sure to put cover back on before starting blender again.)

3 Put dip in serving bowl. Sprinkle with sunflower seeds, if you like.

4 Serve with any of these vegetable "dippers" - - - - - - - - ➤

> **Carrot sticks**
> **Celery sticks**
> **Cucumber slices**
> **Small chunks of broccoli**
> **Small chunks of cauliflower**
> **Your favorite raw vegetable**

Nutrition Per Tablespoon: Calories 25 (Calories from Fat 10); Fat 1g (Saturated 1g); Cholesterol 5mg; Sodium 150mg; Carbohydrate 2g (Dietary Fiber 0g); Protein 2g

◂◂◂◂◂ FISH AND STICKS ▸▸▸▸▸

About 36 cookies

Utensils You Will Need

2 cookie sheets • Pastry brush • 3-quart saucepan • Dry-ingredient measuring cup • Measuring spoon • Wooden spoon • Tablespoon

1 Grease cookie sheets with ‑ ‑ ‑ ‑ ‑ ▸ | **Shortening**

2 Heat in saucepan over low heat, stirring all the time, until melted and smooth ‑ ‑ ‑ ‑ ‑ ‑ ‑ ▸ | **1 cup butterscotch-flavored chips**
1 tablespoon shortening

3 Remove saucepan from heat.

4 Stir in until well coated ‑ ‑ ‑ ‑ ‑ ▸ | **1 package (6 ounces) tiny fish-shaped crackers (about 3 1/2 cups)**
1 cup broken pretzel sticks

5 Drop cracker mixture by rounded tablespoonfuls onto cookie sheets. Let stand about 1 hour or until firm. Carefully remove from cookie sheets.

Nutrition Per Cookie: Calories 50 (Calories from Fat 20); Fat 2g (Saturated 1g); Cholesterol 5mg; Sodium 60mg; Carbohydrate 8g (Dietary Fiber 0g); Protein 0g

Jamie knows a good thing when she tastes it. She says, "I would like to make it again so I could have it in my lunch every day."

HOMEMADE
▲▲▲▲▲ GRANOLA BARS ▲▲▲▲▲

24 bars

Utensils You Will Need

Square pan, 9 × 9 × 2 inches • Pastry brush • 3-quart saucepan •
Dry-ingredient measuring cup • Small sharp knife • Liquid measuring cup •
Measuring spoons • Wooden spoon

1 Grease square pan with ▬ ▬ ▬ ▬ ▬ ➤ | **Shortening**

2 Heat in saucepan over medium heat,
stirring all the time, until boiling ▬ ▬ ➤

1/4 cup sugar
1/4 cup (1/2 stick) margarine or butter
1/3 cup honey
1/2 teaspoon ground cinnamon

3 Boil sugar mixture 1 minute, stirring all
the time. Remove saucepan from heat.

4 Stir in ▬ ▬ ▬ ▬ ▬ ▬ ▬ ▬ ▬ ➤

1 cup diced dried fruits and raisins

5 Stir in ━ ━ ━ ━ ━ ━ ━ ━ ━ ━ ➤

> **1 1/2 cups whole-grain wheat flake cereal**
> **1 cup quick-cooking oats**
> **1/2 cup sliced almonds**

6 Press mixture in pan with back of wooden spoon. Cool completely. Cut mixture into 2 1/4 × 1 1/2-inch bars.

Nutrition Per Bar: Calories 85 (Calories from Fat 25); Fat 3g (Saturated 1g); Cholesterol 0mg; Sodium 40mg; Carbohydrate 14g (Dietary Fiber 1g); Protein 1g

Max gave his mom a special treat when he served the bars he made himself to her on Mother's Day.

HINT
Put pan in refrigerator to speed up cooling.

FROZEN "YOGONANAS"

4 servings

Utensils You Will Need

Waxed paper • Dinner plate • Plastic bag with zipper top • Rolling pin •
Dry-ingredient measuring cups • Knife • Cutting board •
4 flat wooden ice-cream sticks • Shallow bowl

1 Put piece of waxed paper on dinner plate.

2 Put in plastic bag – – – – – – → | 1 cup honey graham cereal |

3 Press air out of plastic bag, then seal. Roll cereal with rolling pin or jar until crushed.

4 Peel, then cut crosswise in half – – – → | 2 large bananas |

5 Carefully poke a wooden stick into the cut end of each banana half.

6 Put in shallow bowl – – – – – – → | 1/2 cup plain or flavored yogurt |

7 Roll each banana half in the yogurt, then sprinkle with some of the crushed cereal. Put "yogonanas" on the plate. Freeze about 2 hours or until "yogonanas" are hard. Keep frozen until served.

Nutrition Per Serving: Calories 117 (Calories from Fat 10); Fat 1g (Saturated 1g); Cholesterol 5mg; Sodium 100mg; Carbohydrate 25g (Dietary Fiber 1g); Protein 3g

Frozen "Yogonanas," Pineapple Fizz (page 73)

FROZEN TROPICAL
▲▲▲▲▲ DREAM POPS ▲▲▲▲▲

7 pops

 Utensils You Will Need

Medium bowl • Dry-ingredient measuring cup • Wooden spoon • 7 three-ounce
paper cups • 7 flat wooden ice-cream sticks

1 Mix in medium bowl with
wooden spoon ▬ ▬ ▬ ▬ ▬ ▬ ▬ ▬ ▶

2 Spoon yogurt mixture into paper cups.

3 Freeze about 45 minutes or until
mixture begins to thicken.

> **2 cups plain yogurt**
> **1/2 cup drained crushed**
> **pineapple**
> **1 can (6 ounces) frozen orange**
> **juice concentrate, thawed**

4 Poke a wooden stick into the center of each pop. Freeze about 4 hours longer
or until pops are solid. Peel the paper cups from the frozen
pops before eating.

*Nutrition Per Pop: Calories 100 (Calories from
Fat 10); Fat 1g (Saturated 1g); Cholesterol 5mg;
Sodium 50mg; Carbohydrate 19g (Dietary Fiber 0g);
Protein 4g*

HINT
*You can also make these
pops without the wooden
sticks. Then, just peel the
paper cup off as you eat
the frozen pop.*

▲▲▲▲ FROSTY FRUITY SODAS ▲▲▲▲

4 servings

Utensils You Will Need

4 short, wide glasses • Liquid measuring cup • Ice-cream scoop • Straws

1 Pour into each glass 1/4 cup of - - → | **1 cup chilled cranberry juice cocktail**

2 Put into each glass 1 small scoop (1/4 cup) of - - - - - - → | **1 cup raspberry sherbet**

3 Fill each glass with 3 ounces of - - → | **12 ounces chilled ginger ale**

4 If you like, sprinkle with colored candies. Serve right away with straw.

Nutrition Per Serving: Calories 140 (Calories from Fat 10); Fat 1g (Saturated 1g); Cholesterol 5mg; Sodium 35mg; Carbohydrate 33g (Dietary Fiber 0g); Protein 0g

Jessie liked the sherbet in this "just plain simple and good" cool drink.

▲▲▲▲▲ **VERY STRAWBERRY SODA** ▲▲▲▲▲

1 soda

Utensils You Will Need

Tall glass • Tablespoon • Measuring spoons • Ice-cream scoop •
Liquid measuring cup • Straw

1 Mix in tall glass with tablespoon - - - ➤

> **2 tablespoons strawberry ice-cream topping
> 2 tablespoons pineapple ice-cream topping
> 1 small scoop (1/4 cup) vanilla ice cream**

2 Stir in - - - - - - - - - - - - ➤

> **1/4 cup chilled strawberry soda pop**

3 Add - - - - - - - - - - - - - ➤

> **3 medium scoops (1 cup) vanilla ice cream**

4 Fill glass with - - - - - - - - ➤

> **Chilled strawberry soda pop**

5 Serve right away with straw.

Nutrition Per Soda: Calories 750 (Calories from Fat 160); Fat 18g (Saturated 11g); Cholesterol 70mg; Sodium 210mg; Carbohydrate 142g (Dietary Fiber 1g); Protein 6g

▲▲▲▲▲ PINEAPPLE FIZZ ▲▲▲▲▲

2 servings *(photo page 69)*

 Utensils You Will Need

Blender • Liquid measuring cup • Ice-cream scoop • 2 tall glasses • Straws

1 Put in blender ▪ ▪ ▪ ▪ ▪ ▪ ▪ ▶

1 1/2 cups pineapple juice
3 medium scoops (1 cup)
pineapple sherbet
1/2 cup sparkling water

2 Cover blender. Blend on low speed about 10 seconds or until mixture is smooth.

3 Pour mixture into glasses. Serve right away with straws.

Nutrition Per Serving: Calories 240 (Calories from Fat 20); Fat 2g (Saturated 1g); Cholesterol 5mg; Sodium 45mg; Carbohydrate 55g (Dietary Fiber 0g); Protein 1g

HINT
To keep your drink cold and refreshing, refrigerate the pineapple juice and sparkling water before using.

HOMEMADE HOT
▲▲▲▲▲ COCOA MIX ▲▲▲▲▲
4 1/2 cups mix

Utensils You Will Need

Large bowl • Dry-ingredient measuring cups • Measuring spoons •
Wooden spoon • Mug • Liquid measuring cup • Spoon

1 Mix in large bowl with
wooden spoon - - - - - →

> 2 2/3 cups nonfat dry
> milk powder
> 1 1/2 cups cocoa
> 1 cup sugar
> 1/4 teaspoon salt

2 Store in tightly covered labeled
container at room temperature up
to 6 months.

3 For each serving, mix in mug until
smooth - - - - - →

> 2 heaping teaspoons Homemade
> Hot Cocoa Mix
> 2 tablespoons cold milk or water

4 Stir in - - - - - →

> 1 cup hot milk or water

5 If you like, top with - - - - - →

> Miniature marshmallows

Nutrition Per Serving: Calories 40 (Calories from Fat 10); Fat 1g (Saturated 1g); Cholesterol 2mg; Sodium 35mg; Carbohydrate 7g (Dietary Fiber 1g); Protein 2g

Rachel's mom thinks this is a great recipe to have on hand and Rachel says, "Putting colored marshmallows on top made it pretty."

HINT
This recipe also makes a great gift. Write the directions for making each serving on a card to give along with the mix.

3

Mini-Meals
and
Sandwiches

Hungry-time Hoagies (page 89)

▲▲▲▲▲ APPLESAUCE YOGURT ▲▲▲▲▲

2 servings

 Utensils You Will Need

Small bowl • Dry-ingredient measuring cup • Measuring spoons •
Wooden spoon • 2 small bowls

1 Mix in small bowl with wooden spoon ⤍ ⤍ ⤍ ⤍ ⤍

> **1 cup vanilla yogurt**
> **1 cup applesauce**
> **1 tablespoon honey**
> **1/4 teaspoon pumpkin pie spice or ground cinnamon**

2 Sprinkle with ⤍ ⤍ ⤍ ⤍ ⤍

> **2 teaspoons chopped pecans**

Here's another idea…Make **Fruity Applesauce Yogurt:** Use your favorite fruit-flavored yogurt in place of the vanilla yogurt.

Nutrition Per Serving: Calories 275 (Calories from Fat 25); Fat 3g (Saturated 1g); Cholesterol 5mg; Sodium 75mg; Carbohydrate 58g (Dietary Fiber 2g); Protein 6g

When Dan served this recipe, he put both pecans and walnuts on top. He also suggests topping it with raisins, chopped peanuts and your favorite cereal.

Crispy Potato Veggies (page 80)

▲▲▲▲▲ CRISPY POTATO VEGGIES ▲▲▲▲▲

4 servings *(photo page 79)*

Utensils You Will Need

2 small bowls • Dry-ingredient measuring cups • Small sharp knife •
Measuring spoons • Spoon • Fork • Slotted spoon • Cookie sheet • Pot holders •
Spatula • Serving plate

1 Heat oven to 400°.

2 Prepare - - - - - - - ▶
> **2 cups fresh vegetables (broccoli flowerets or cauliflowerets, 1/4-inch carrot slices, 2-inch zucchini slices, 1/2-inch strips green or red bell pepper)**

3 Mix in small bowl with spoon - - ▶
> **1/2 cup instant mashed potatoes (dry)**
> **1/4 cup grated Parmesan cheese**
> **2 tablespoons margarine or butter, melted**
> **1/2 teaspoon garlic powder**
> **1/4 teaspoon dried basil leaves**

4 Beat in shallow dish with fork - - ▶
> **1 egg**

5 Put about 1/2 cup of vegetables in beaten egg. Remove vegetables, 1 piece at a time, with slotted spoon, fork or fingers. Roll vegetables in potato mixture until coated. Put vegetables on cookie sheet.

6 Bake 10 to 12 minutes or until light brown. Immediately remove vegetables from cookie sheet with spatula to serving plate.

Nutrition Per Serving: Calories 135 (Calories from Fat 80); Fat 9g (Saturated 3g); Cholesterol 55mg; Sodium 190mg; Carbohydrate 9g (Dietary Fiber 1g); Protein 5g

HINT
You can buy cut-up vegetables at the salad bar or produce section at the supermarket.

Jared labeled this a healthy food because it's a vegetable—and it's delicious!

▲▲▲▲ HARD-COOKED EGGS ▲▲▲▲

🍴 Utensil You Will Need

Saucepan with lid

1 Put in saucepan – – – – – – –▶

Desired number of eggs

2 Add enough cold water to saucepan to come at least 1 inch above the eggs.

3 Heat water rapidly to boiling, then remove saucepan from heat. Cover and let stand 18 minutes.

4 Run cold water into the saucepan to quickly cool the eggs and keep them from cooking more.

5 Tap each egg on the kitchen counter to crack the shell. Roll egg between your hands to loosen the shell, then peel. Hold egg under running water to help rinse off the shell.

6 Or store eggs in their shell in the refrigerator for up to 1 week.

Nutrition Per Egg: Calories 70 (Calories from Fat 45); Fat 5g (Saturated 2g); Cholesterol 215mg; Sodium 60mg; Carbohydrate 0g (Dietary Fiber 0g); Protein 6g

DEVILED EGGS ▲▲▲▲ WITH VEGGIES ▲▲▲▲

4 servings

 **Utensils You Will Need**

Sharp knife • Small bowl • Fork • Measuring spoons • Cutting board •
Wooden spoon • Teaspoon

1 Adult help: Peel, then cut length-wise in half ▪ ▪ ▪ ▪ ▪ ▪ ▶ | **4 Hard-cooked Eggs (page 82)**

2 Slip egg yolks out of egg whites. Mash egg yolks in small bowl with fork.

3 Mix in ▪ ▪ ▪ ▪ ▪ ▪ ▪ ▪ ▶ | **2 tablespoons plain yogurt or sour cream**
2 tablespoons finely chopped zucchini
1 tablespoon finely chopped celery
1 teaspoon chopped fresh dill weed or 1/4 teaspoon dried dill weed
1/4 teaspoon prepared mustard
1/4 teaspoon salt
1/8 teaspoon pepper

4 Fill egg whites with egg yolk mixture, mounding it lightly.

5 If you like, sprinkle eggs with ▪ ▪ ▪ ▶ | **Paprika**

6 Cover and refrigerate eggs up to 24 hours.

Nutrition Per Serving: Calories 75 (Calories from Fat 45); Fat 5g (Saturated 2g); Cholesterol 210mg; Sodium 210mg; Carbohydrate 1g (Dietary Fiber 0g); Protein 7g

▲▲▲▲▲ SLOPPY FRANKS ▲▲▲▲▲

8 sandwiches

Utensils You Will Need

10-inch skillet • Measuring spoon • Cutting board • Sharp knife • Dry-ingredient measuring cups • Wooden spoon • Liquid measuring cup • Can opener

1 Heat in skillet until hot ‑ ‑ ‑ ‑ ➔ | **2 tablespoons vegetable oil**

2 Cook in oil, stirring a few times, until onion is tender ‑ ‑ ‑ ‑ ‑ ➔ | **1/2 cup chopped green bell pepper**
1/3 cup chopped onion

3 Stir in, then simmer uncovered 10 minutes, stirring a few times ‑ ‑ ‑ ➔ | **1/2 cup barbecue sauce**
1 can (8 ounces) tomato sauce
1 pound hot dogs, cut into 1/4-inch slices

4 Fill with sloppy frank mixture ‑ ‑ ➔ | **8 hot dog or hamburger buns, split**

Nutrition Per Sandwich: Calories 360 (Calories from Fat 205); Fat 23g (Saturated 7g); Cholesterol 30mg; Sodium 1180mg; Carbohydrate 29g (Dietary Fiber 2g); Protein 11g

Shawyn loves hot dogs and liked this recipe because "These were pretty close to BBQ dogs minus the grill."

PEANUTTY APPLE
▲▲▲▲▲ SANDWICHES ▲▲▲▲▲

4 sandwiches

 **Utensils You Will Need**

Small bowl • Dry-ingredient measuring cups • Measuring spoons •
Wooden spoon • Knife • Sharp knife

1 Mix in small bowl with
wooden spoon - - - - - - - ➤

> **3/4 cup chunky peanut butter**
> **1/4 cup apricot preserves**
> **1/2 teaspoon ground mustard**

2 Spread peanut butter mixture on - - ➤

> **4 slices raisin bread**

3 Put on peanut butter mixture - - - ➤

> **2 medium peeled or unpeeled**
> **eating apples, thinly sliced**
> **Lettuce leaves**

4 Top with - - - - - - - - - ➤

> **4 slices raisin bread**

*Nutrition Per Sandwich: Calories 525 (Calories from Fat 245); Fat 27g (Saturated 5g);
Cholesterol 0mg; Sodium 440mg; Carbohydrate 61g (Dietary Fiber 7g); Protein 16g*

**According to Max, "There was a lot of peanut
butter in it, and that means it was Excellent!!!"**

VEGETABLE PATCH PITA SANDWICHES

4 sandwiches

 **Utensils You Will Need**

Medium bowl • Wooden spoon • Sharp knife • Cutting board •
Dry-ingredient measuring cups • Measuring spoons • Teaspoon

1 Mix in medium bowl with wooden spoon - - - - - ▶

> **3 cups bite-size cut-up fresh vegetables (cauliflower, broccoli, carrots, green bell pepper, green onion, cherry tomatoes or zucchini)**
> **1/2 cup mayonnaise or salad dressing**
> **1 teaspoon prepared mustard**

2 Cut crosswise in half - - - - - ▶

> **4 pita breads (about 6 inches across)**

3 Open "pocket" in each pita bread half. Spoon about 1/3 cup of the vegetable mixture into each pocket.

4 If you like, put in each pocket 1 of - ▶

> **8 pieces lettuce**

Nutrition Per Sandwich: Calories 385 (Calories from Fat 205); Fat 23g (Saturated 1g); Cholesterol 15mg; Sodium 520mg; Carbohydrate 40g (Dietary Fiber 3g); Protein 7g

Vegetable Patch Pita Sandwiches

▲▲▲▲▲EGG SALAD SANDWICHES▲▲▲▲▲

4 sandwiches

Utensils You Will Need

Sharp knife • Cutting board • Medium bowl • Spoon • Measuring spoons • Knife

1 Adult help: Peel, then chop into small pieces ─ ─ ─ ─ ─ ─ ─ ─ ─ ➤ **3 Hard-cooked Eggs (page 82)**

2 Wash, then chop into very small pieces ─ ─ ─ ─ ─ ─ ─ ─ ─ ─ ➤ **1 stalk celery**

3 Put chopped eggs and celery in medium bowl.

4 Stir in ─ ─ ─ ─ ─ ─ ─ ─ ─ ─ ─ ➤ **3 tablespoons mayonnaise or salad dressing**
1/4 teaspoon onion salt

5 Spread egg mixture on 4 slices of the bread. Top with the other 4 slices. ─ ─ ─ ─ ─ ─ ─ ─ ➤ **8 slices bread**

6 Cut each sandwich in half. Serve right away. Wrap and refrigerate any leftover sandwiches.

Nutrition Per Sandwich: Calories 300 (Calories from Fat 160); Fat 18g (Saturated 4g); Cholesterol 170mg; Sodium 530mg; Carbohydrate 26g (Dietary Fiber 1g); Protein 9

▲▲▲▲ HUNGRY-TIME HOAGIES ▲▲▲▲

6 sandwiches *(photo page 77)*

 **Utensils You Will Need**

Sharp knife • Cutting board • Knife

1 Adult help: If not already split, cut ■▶ | **6 hoagie or hot dog buns**

2 Spread buns with ▬ ▬ ▬ ▬ ▬ ▬▶ | **Mayonnaise or salad dressing**

3 Adult help: Wash, then cut into slices ▬ ▬ ▬ ▬ ▬ ▬ ▬▶ | **2 medium tomatoes**

4 Put on bottom of each bun ▬ ▬ ▬▶ | **2 or 3 slices ham, luncheon meat or roast beef**
1 slice cheese
2 slices of the tomatoes
1 piece lettuce

5 Replace tops of buns. Cut hoagies crosswise in half, if you like.

Nutrition Per Sandwich: Calories 340 (Calories from Fat 155); Fat 17g (Saturated 6g); Cholesterol 45mg; Sodium 1080mg; Carbohydrate 31g (Dietary Fiber 2g); Protein 18g

DINOSAUR BIRTHDAY PARTY

Dinosaurs live—in the hearts and minds of kids anyway! Treat your friends to a panorama of the giant prehistoric creatures on your birthday. Decorate the table with dinosaur figures and use dinosaur paper plates and napkins, if you like. The dinosaur-shaped molds are available at many discount, specialty and department stores. Eight-ounce custard cups can be used if you don't have the molds. Follow the Easy Plan below for a birthday party that takes you back in time.

Menu

Dinosaur Calzones   page 108

Fruity Gelatin Molds   page 136

Carrot Sticks

Dinosaur Cakes   page 144

Ice Cream

Easy Party Plan

1 Several days before the party, make up a shopping list from the menu and recipes and buy the ingredients that you need.

2 The day before, bake the cake for the Dinosaur Cakes and make the Fruity Gelatin Molds. Cut the carrots into sticks and refrigerate in a sealed plastic bag.

3 The morning of the party, cut out and decorate the cakes.

4 During the party, ask an adult to make the meat mixture and dough for the Dinosaur Calzones. Divide your friends into 2 teams and have each team make a dinosaur.

Dinosaur Calzones, Fruity Gelatin Molds, Dinosaur Cakes

▲▲▲▲▲TUNA MELT BURGERS▲▲▲▲▲

6 sandwiches

Utensils You Will Need

Medium bowl • Can opener • Fork • Cutting board • Sharp knife •
Dry-ingredient measuring cups • Measuring spoons • Wooden spoon • Knife •
Spoon • Aluminum foil • Cookie sheet • Pot holders

1 Heat oven to 350°.

2 Drain in colander, then break apart
with fork - - - - - - - - - ➤

1 can (6 1/8 ounces) tuna

3 Mix in medium bowl with
wooden spoon - - - - - - - ➤

The tuna
2 medium stalks celery, chopped (1 cup)
1/2 cup diced process American cheese
1/4 cup mayonnaise or salad dressing
1 tablespoon instant minced onion
1/4 teaspoon salt
1/8 teaspoon pepper

4 Spread tuna mixture on bottoms of ➤

6 hamburger buns, split

5 Replace tops of buns. Put each sandwich
on a square of aluminum foil, then wrap foil around sandwiches, folding
edges securely.

6 Bake about 20 minutes or until hot in middle. Cool slightly before serving.

Nutrition Per Sandwich: Calories 255 (Calories from Fat 115); Fat 13g (Saturated 4g); Cholesterol 25mg; Sodium 570mg; Carbohydrate 23g (Dietary Fiber 1g); Protein 13g

HINT
Tuna Melt Burgers can be made, wrapped and refrigerated up to 8 hours ahead of time. Increase bake time to about 30 minutes.

Jared added sweet pickles to his version and said that everybody liked it. His mom thought it was great having Jared prepare the meal!

TOASTY HOT DOG
▲▲▲▲▲ **ROLL-UPS** ▲▲▲▲▲

8 roll-ups *(photo page 96)*

❦ Utensils You Will Need

1-quart saucepan • Cookie sheet • Pastry brush • Knife • Tongs •
Toothpicks • Pot holders

1 Heat oven to 375°.

2 Melt in saucepan over low heat - - - ➤ | **1/2 cup (1 stick) margarine or butter**

3 Put on cookie sheet - - - - - - ➤ | **8 slices bread**

4 Brush about half the melted margarine over bread slices, using pastry brush.

5 Spread with - - - - - - - - ➤ | **2 teaspoons prepared mustard**

6 Cut in half so you have 8 cheese triangles, then put 1 triangle on each slice of bread - - - - - ➤ | **4 slices processed American cheese**

7 Put on each cheese triangle 1 of - - ➤ | **8 hot dogs**

8 Fold each slice of bread over the hot dog and cheese to make a triangle shape. Fasten with 2 toothpicks, one on each side, poking them through the bread and hot dog. Brush the outsides of the bread triangles with the rest of the melted margarine.

9 Bake 10 to 15 minutes or until golden brown.

10 Serve with ━ ━ ━ ━ ━ ━ ━ ➤

Ketchup

Nutrition Per Roll-up: Calories 355 (Calories from Fat 260); Fat 29g (Saturated 9g); Cholesterol 35mg; Sodium 940mg; Carbohydrate 14g (Dietary Fiber 0g); Protein 9g

HINT
Softer breads work best for this recipe. Coarser breads tend to break instead of folding.

▲▲▲▲▲ LITTLE LUNCH PIZZA ▲▲▲▲▲

1 pizza

Utensils You Will Need

Fork • Toaster • Cookie sheet • Measuring spoons • Pot holders • Spatula

1 Heat oven to 425°.

2 Split with fork, then toast – – – ➤ | **1 English muffin** |

3 Put muffin halves on cookie sheet.

4 Top each muffin half with – – – ➤ | **1 tablespoon pizza sauce**
 1 tablespoon shredded Cheddar
 or mozzarella cheese |

5 Bake about 5 minutes or until cheese is melted. Remove muffin halves from cookie sheet with spatula. Cool slightly.

To Microwave:

Split and toast English muffins, then top with pizza sauce and cheese as directed in step 4.

Put microwavable paper towel on microwavable plate. Put muffin halves on the paper towel. Microwave uncovered on High (100%) 30 to 45 seconds or until cheese is melted. Cool slightly.

Here's another idea…Make **Hearty Lunch Pizza:** Add some crumbled cooked hamburger, sliced pepperoni, sliced olives, chopped tomato or your favorite topping on the pizza sauce before putting on the cheese.

Nutrition Per Pizza: Calories 160 (Calories from Fat 35); Fat 4g (Saturated 2g); Cholesterol 10mg; Sodium 370mg; Carbohydrate 27g (Dietary Fiber 2g); Protein 6g

Toasty Hot Dog Roll-ups (page 94)

▲▲▲▲▲ **REUBEN PITAS** ▲▲▲▲▲

4 sandwiches

Utensils You Will Need

Cutting board • Sharp knife • Medium bowl • Can opener • Dry-ingredient measuring cups • Liquid measuring cup • Measuring spoon • Wooden spoon • Cookie sheet • Spatula

1 Heat oven to 425°.

2 Adult help: Cut in half around edge with knife ▬ ▬ ▬ ▬ ▬ ▬ ▶

> **2 pita breads (about 6 inches across)**

3 Mix in medium bowl with wooden spoon ▬ ▬ ▬ ▬ ▬ ▬ ▶

> **6 ounces thinly sliced corned beef, coarsely chopped**
> **1 can (8 ounces) sauerkraut, rinsed and well drained**
> **1 cup shredded Swiss cheese (4 ounces)**
> **1/3 cup Thousand Island dressing**
> **2 teaspoons caraway seed, if you like**

4 Spread beef mixture on pita bread halves. Put on cookie sheet.

5 Bake 5 to 7 minutes or until cheese is melted. Remove sandwiches from cookie sheet with spatula.

To Microwave:

Put sandwiches in a circle on microwavable rack. Cover with a microwavable paper towel.

Microwave on Medium (50%) 2 minutes. Turn the dish 1/2 turn. Microwave on Medium (50%) 2 to 3 minutes longer or until filling is hot and cheese is melted.

Nutrition Per Sandwich: Calories 365 (Calories from Fat 205); Fat 23g (Saturated 9g); Cholesterol 70mg; Sodium 1230mg; Carbohydrate 23g (Dietary Fiber 3g); Protein 19g

This is for the Reuben sandwich lover! When Adam tested this recipe he said, "It was fun serving it to my dad."

▲▲▲▲▲ CHICKEN NOODLE SOUP ▲▲▲▲▲

4 servings

♔♀♬ Utensils You Will Need

3-quart saucepan • Can opener • Wooden spoon •
Dry-ingredient measuring cup • Kitchen scissors

1 Adult help: Make as directed on
cans, then heat to boiling ‒ ‒ ‒ ‒ →

> **2 cans (10 1/2 ounces each)
> condensed chicken broth**

2 Add ‒ ‒ ‒ ‒ ‒ ‒ ‒ ‒ ‒ ‒ →

3 Cook over medium-high heat
6 to 8 minutes or until noodles
are tender.

> **2 cups uncooked egg noodles
> or other pasta**

4 Rinse, then snip with scissors ‒ ‒ ‒ →

> **1 tablespoon lightly packed
> fresh parsley**

5 Just before serving soup, stir in
parsley and ‒ ‒ ‒ ‒ ‒ ‒ ‒ ‒ →

6 Serve with crackers, if you like.

> **1 cup cut-up cooked chicken or
> 1 can (about 6 ounces) chunk
> chicken, drained**

*Nutrition Per Serving: Calories 175 (Calories from Fat 45); Fat 5g (Saturated 1g); Cholesterol 50mg;
Sodium 980mg; Carbohydrate 15g (Dietary Fiber 1g); Protein 19g*

▲▲▲▲▲ VERY VEGETABLE SOUP ▲▲▲▲▲

6 servings

🍴 Utensils You Will Need

3-quart saucepan • Wooden spoon • Can opener • Kitchen scissors •
Measuring spoons • Dry-ingredient measuring cup

1 Mix in saucepan with wooden spoon ▸

> **1 can (10 1/2 ounces) condensed chicken broth
> 1 soup can of water
> 1 can (14 1/2 ounces) stewed tomatoes, undrained
> 1 package (10 ounces) frozen mixed vegetables, separated
> 1/4 teaspoon dried oregano leaves
> 1/4 teaspoon dried thyme leaves
> 1/8 teaspoon pepper**

2 Break up the tomatoes with spoon.

3 Adult help: Heat mixture to boiling. Turn heat down to low. Simmer uncovered 10 minutes.

4 Stir in ▸

> **1/2 cup uncooked macaroni rings or other pasta**

5 Cook about 8 minutes or until macaroni is tender.

To Microwave:

Mix all ingredients except the macaroni in 3-quart microwavable casserole. Cover casserole with lid or plastic wrap. If using plastic wrap, turn back 1 edge to make a little space for the steam to come out.

Microwave on High (100%) 5 minutes. Carefully remove lid, then stir. Re-cover and microwave on High (100%) 8 to 10 minutes or until boiling. Carefully remove lid. Stir in macaroni. Re-cover and microwave on High (100%) 6 to 8 minutes longer or until macaroni is tender.

Nutrition Per Serving: Calories 110 (Calories from Fat 25); Fat 3g (Saturated 1g); Cholesterol 0mg; Sodium 510mg; Carbohydrate 19g (Dietary Fiber 3g); Protein 5g

▲▲▲▲▲ BUNNY SALADS ▲▲▲▲▲

4 salads

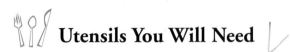 **Utensils You Will Need**

Paper towel • 4 salad plates • Can opener • Small knife • Measuring spoon

1 Wash, then pat dry with paper towel and put on each salad plate 1 of ━ ▶

> **4 lettuce leaves or shredded lettuce**

2 Put on each lettuce leaf, with cut side down, 1 of ━ ━ ━ ━ ━ ━ ▶

> **4 canned pear halves**

3 To make bunny faces, you will need ▪ ▶

> **20 sliced almonds**
> **8 raisins**
> **4 red cinnamon candies**

4 Put on the narrow end of each pear half to make a bunny face: 2 sliced almonds each topped with 1 raisin for eyes, 1 cinnamon candy for nose, 1 sliced almond with tip cut off for teeth and 2 sliced almonds for ears, as shown in the drawing.

5 Put at rounded end of each pear half for bunny tail 2 tablespoons of ━ ━ ▶

> **1/2 cup cottage cheese**

Nutrition Per Salad: Calories 65 (Calories from Fat 25); Fat 3g (Saturated 1g); Cholesterol 5mg; Sodium 110mg; Carbohydrate 8g (Dietary Fiber 2g); Protein 4g

4

Dinnertime Dishes

Smiling Face Pizzas (page 106)

▲▲▲▲▲ SMILING FACE PIZZAS ▲▲▲▲▲

4 pizzas

Utensils You Will Need

Liquid measuring cup • Can opener • Medium bowl • Fork • Dry-ingredient measuring cup • Measuring spoons • Jelly roll pan, 15 1/2 × 10 1/2 × 1 inch • Ruler • Rubber scraper • Sharp knife • Cutting board • Pot holders

1 Heat oven to 425°.

2 Measure out 1/2 cup, then save the rest of ▬ ▬ ▬ ▬ ▬ ▬ ▶

> **1 can (8 ounces) tomato sauce**

3 Mix with fork in medium bowl ▬ ▬ ▬ ▶

> **The 1/2 cup tomato sauce**
> **1 pound ground beef**
> **1/2 cup dry bread crumbs**
> **1/2 teaspoon dried oregano leaves**

4 Divide the beef mixture into 4 equal parts. Put the 4 parts several inches apart in jelly roll pan. Pat each part into 4 1/2-inch circle. Pinch the edge of each circle to make a short rim that stands up. Pour about 2 tablespoons of the saved tomato sauce into the center of each circle. Spread the sauce to the edge of each circle with rubber scraper.

5 Adult help: Bake 15 to 20 minutes. Remove pizzas from oven, then turn off oven.

6 To make faces, you will need ▬ ▬ ▬ ▶

> **1/2 cup shredded mozzarella cheese (2 ounces)**
> **1/4 cup shredded Cheddar cheese (1 ounce)**
> **8 slices ripe olives**
> **4 slices pimiento**

7 Sprinkle mozzarella cheese over pizzas for face. Sprinkle Cheddar cheese around top edge for hair. Put on olive slices for eyes and pimiento slices for mouths. Heat pizzas in warm oven about 5 minutes or until cheese is melted.

Nutrition Per Pizza: Calories 370 (Calories from Fat 200); Fat 22g (Saturated 10g); Cholesterol 80mg; Sodium 640mg; Carbohydrate 15g (Dietary Fiber 1g); Protein 29g

HINT
You can use your favorite foods to make the faces. Try broccoli for ears, alfalfa sprouts for hair, mushroom slices for eyebrows, cherry tomato halves for noses. Be creative!

▲▲▲▲▲ DINOSAUR CALZONES ▲▲▲▲▲

10 servings *(photo page 91)*

Utensils You Will Need

10-inch skillet • Wooden spoon • Colander • Cutting board • Sharp knife •
Dry-ingredient measuring cup • Liquid measuring cup • Large bowl •
Measuring spoons • Rolling pin • Ruler • 2 cookie sheets • Small bowl • Fork •
Pastry brush • Pot holders

1 Heat oven to 450°.

2 Adult help: Cook in skillet over medium heat about 10 minutes, stirring often, until brown - - - - ▶

> **1 pound ground beef**

3 Pour beef into colander to drain off any fat. Put beef back in skillet.

4 Stir into beef, then set aside - - - ▶

> **1 medium onion, chopped (1/2 cup)**
> **2/3 cup pizza sauce**

5 Mix in large bowl to make a dough (using hands to shape into ball, if necessary) - - - - - - ▶

> **5 cups Bisquick Original baking mix**
> **3/4 cup water**
> **3 tablespoons vegetable oil**

6 Cut off and save about 1/4 of the dough. Divide the rest of the dough in half.

7 Sprinkle a clean surface (such as a kitchen counter or breadboard) with flour or baking mix. Put dough on surface. Roll or pat each dough half into 12-inch circle. Put each circle on cookie sheet.

8 Top half of each circle (1/2 cup for each circle) - - - - - - - ▶

> **1 cup shredded Cheddar cheese (4 ounces)**

9 Top cheese with beef mixture to within 1 inch of edge of dough. Fold dough over filling, then press edge with fork to seal.

10 Beat in small bowl with fork ━ ━ ━ ━▶ | **1 egg white** |

11 Make fourteen 3/4-inch balls from some of the saved dough. Press 10 of the balls into triangle shapes. Press 5 triangles into sealed edge of each calzone for spikes on the backs of the dinosaurs, using egg white as glue. (Use the photo on page 90 as a guide.)

12 Roll the rest of the balls between your hands to make legs with feet. Press 2 legs into folded edge of each calzone, using egg white as glue. Divide the rest of the saved dough into 4 pieces. Roll pieces between your hands to make tails and heads with necks. Press into calzones, using egg white as glue.

13 If you like, press into each head for eye 1 of ━ ━ ━ ━ ━ ━ ━ ━ ━▶ | **2 whole peppercorns** |

14 Bake 15 to 20 minutes or until golden brown (it may be necessary to cover small dough pieces with pieces of aluminum foil during the last few minutes of baking).

Nutrition Per Serving: Calories 425 (Calories from Fat 205); Fat 23g (Saturated 8g); Cholesterol 40mg; Sodium 1020mg; Carbohydrate 39g (Dietary Fiber 1g); Protein 16g

HINT
If your oven does not hold 2 cookie sheets side by side, make one calzone with half the dough and beef mixture. Bake that one while you make the second calzone.

Dan had fun making the calzone look like a dinosaur and thinks it would be neat made into a Tyrannosaurus Rex. And besides, "It makes a good dinner."

▲▲▲▲▲ QUICK CHEESEBURGER PIE ▲▲▲▲▲

6 servings

♈ Utensils You Will Need

Pie plate, 10 × 1 1/2 inches • Pastry brush • Sharp knife • Cutting board •
10-inch skillet • Wooden spoon • Measuring spoons • Strainer • Blender •
Liquid measuring cup • Dry-ingredient measuring cups • Pot holders • Knife

1 Heat oven to 400°.

2 Grease pie plate with — — — — — → | **Shortening** |

3 Adult help: Wash, then chop with sharp knife — — — — — → | **2 medium onions** |

4 Cook in skillet over medium heat about 10 minutes, stirring often, until beef is brown — — — — → | **The chopped onions**
 1 pound ground beef
 1/4 teaspoon pepper |

5 Pour beef mixture into strainer to drain off any fat. Spread beef mixture in pie plate.

6 Put in blender, cover and blend on high speed 15 seconds (or use eggbeater or wire whisk), then pour over beef in pie plate — — — — → | **1 1/2 cups milk**
 3 large eggs
 3/4 cup Bisquick Original baking mix |

7 Bake 25 minutes.

8 Adult help: Meanwhile, wash, then cut into slices — — — — → | **2 medium tomatoes** |

9 Adult help: Carefully remove pie from oven. Top with tomatoes, then sprinkle with ▪ ▪ ▪ ▪ ▪ ▪ ▪ ▪ ▪ ➤

> **1 cup shredded Cheddar or process American cheese (4 ounces)**

10 Bake 5 to 8 minutes longer or until knife poked in center of pie comes out clean. Cool 5 minutes.

To Microwave:

Break ground beef into small pieces in microwavable pie plate, 10 × 1 1/2 inches. Top with chopped onions. Cover with waxed paper. (Put waxed paper on pie plate so it curls down instead of up. It will stay on better.)

Microwave on High (100%) 3 minutes. Carefully remove waxed paper, then stir. Re-cover and microwave on High (100%) 3 to 4 minutes longer or until beef is brown. Pour beef mixture into strainer to drain off any fat. Put beef mixture back in pie plate.

Follow step 6 above to prepare topping for pie. Put pie plate on a microwavable dinner plate turned upside down in the microwave. Microwave uncovered on Medium-high (70%) 6 minutes. Turn pie plate 1/4 turn. Microwave 6 to 12 minutes longer or until a knife poked in center comes out clean.

Follow steps 8 and 9 above to top pie with tomato slices and cheese. Microwave uncovered on Medium-high (70%) 3 minutes. Turn pie plate 1/4 turn. Microwave on Medium-high (70%) 3 to 5 minutes longer or until cheese is melted.

Adult help: Carefully take pie out of microwave oven. Let pie stand on a flat, heat-proof surface for 5 minutes. (Do not put on a wire cooling rack.)

Nutrition Per Serving: Calories 375 (Calories from Fat 205); Fat 23g (Saturated 10g); Cholesterol 175mg; Sodium 430mg; Carbohydrate 18g (Dietary Fiber 1g); Protein 25g

▲▲▲▲▲ FIESTA CHILI ▲▲▲▲▲

4 to 6 servings

Utensils You Will Need

Sharp knife • Cutting board • 3-quart saucepan • Wooden spoon • Strainer • Measuring spoons • Can opener

1 Adult help: Wash, then chop with sharp knife ---➤

> **1 medium onion**

2 Cook in saucepan over medium heat about 10 minutes, stirring often, until brown ---➤

> **The chopped onion**
> **1 pound ground beef**

3 Pour beef mixture into strainer to drain off any fat. Put beef mixture back in saucepan.

4 Stir into beef mixture ---➤

> **1 tablespoon chili powder**
> **1/2 teaspoon garlic salt**
> **Dash of red pepper sauce**
> **1 can (14 1/2 ounces) whole tomatoes, undrained**

5 Heat mixture to boiling. Turn heat down to low. Simmer uncovered 30 minutes, stirring a few times.

6 Stir in ---➤

> **1 can (15 to 16 ounces) red kidney beans, undrained**

7 Simmer 30 minutes longer.

8 Top each serving with ---➤

> **1 or 2 tablespoons shredded Cheddar cheese**

To Microwave:

Break ground beef into small pieces in 3-quart microwavable casserole or bowl. Top with chopped onion. Cover with waxed paper. (Put waxed paper on casserole so it curls down instead of up. It will stay on better.)

Microwave on High (100%) 3 minutes. Carefully remove waxed paper, then stir. Re-cover and microwave on High (100%) 3 to 4 minutes longer or until brown.

Pour beef mixture into strainer to drain off any fat. Put beef mixture back in casserole. Stir in tomatoes, breaking them up with a fork. Stir in kidney beans (with the liquid in the can), chili powder, garlic salt and red pepper sauce.

Cover with lid or plastic wrap. If using plastic wrap, turn back 1 edge to make a little space for the steam to come out. Microwave on High (100%) 10 minutes. Carefully remove lid, then stir. Re-cover and microwave on High (100%) 8 to 10 minutes longer or until mixture is slightly thickened.

Nutrition Per Serving: Calories 340 (Calories from Fat 160); Fat 18g (Saturated 7g); Cholesterol 65mg; Sodium 690mg; Carbohydrate 23g (Dietary Fiber 7g); Protein 28g

▴▴▴▴▴ JUICY HAMBURGERS ▴▴▴▴▴

6 hamburgers

 **Utensils You Will Need**

Sharp knife • Cutting board • Medium bowl • Fork • Liquid measuring cup •
Measuring spoons • Ruler • Broiler pan • Spatula

1 Adult help: Wash, then chop - - - ➤ | **1 small onion**

2 Mix in medium bowl with fork - - ➤

3 Shape beef mixture with your
hands into 6 burgers, each about
3/4 inch thick. Put burgers on
rack in broiler pan.

> **The chopped onion**
> **1 1/2 pounds ground beef**
> **1/4 cup water**
> **1 teaspoon Worcestershire sauce**
> **1/4 teaspoon salt**
> **1/4 teaspoon pepper**

4 Adult help: Set oven control to broil. Broil burgers with tops about 3 inches
from heat 5 minutes. Turn burgers over with spatula. Broil 5 to 7 minutes
longer or until no longer pink in center.

Here's another idea…Make **Cheeseburgers:** Put 1 slice process American cheese on each
burger during the last minute of broiling.

*Nutrition Per Hamburger: Calories 230 (Calories from Fat 145); Fat 16g (Saturated 7g); Cholesterol 65mg;
Sodium 150mg; Carbohydrate 1g (Dietary Fiber 0g); Protein 21g*

Glazed Roast Chicken (page 116)

GLAZED ROAST CHICKEN

6 servings *(photo page 115)*

Utensils You Will Need

Paper towels • Shallow roasting pan with rack • 1-quart saucepan •
Liquid measuring cup • Measuring spoons • Cutting board • Sharp knife •
Pastry brush • Meat thermometer • Pot holders

1 Heat oven to 375°.

2 Rinse, then pat dry with
paper towels ------➤ **2 1/2- to 3-pound whole broiler-fryer chicken**

3 Fold chicken's wings behind its
back, with the tips touching. Tie
drumsticks together, or skewer them
to the tail. Put chicken, breast side
up, on rack in roasting pan.

4 Melt in saucepan over low heat --➤ **1/2 cup (1 stick) margarine or butter**

5 Stir in ------➤ **1/4 cup lemon juice
2 tablespoons honey
2 teaspoons dried rosemary
leaves, crushed
1 clove garlic, finely chopped**

6 Adult help: Insert meat thermometer in
thigh muscle so thermometer does not
touch bone. Brush margarine mixture
over chicken.

7 Roast uncovered 1 to 1 1/4 hours, brushing chicken several times with remaining margarine mixture, until thermometer reads 180° and juice of chicken is no longer pink when center of thigh is cut.

Nutrition Per Serving: Calories 385 (Calories from Fat 245); Fat 27g (Saturated 7g); Cholesterol 85mg; Sodium 260mg; Carbohydrate 7g (Dietary Fiber 0g); Protein 28g

HINT
The clove of garlic also can be pressed through a garlic press instead of finely chopped.

When Jamie served this tasty chicken recipe to her family she felt like she had prepared a "real" meal.

▲▲▲▲ OVEN-FRIED CHICKEN ▲▲▲▲

6 servings

Utensils You Will Need

Rectangular pan, 13 × 9 × 2 inches • Plastic bag with zipper top •
Small sharp knife • Pot holders • Plastic bag • Dry-ingredient measuring cup •
Measuring spoons • Tongs

1 Heat oven to 425°.

2 Adult help: Heat in rectangular
pan in oven until melted, then
remove pan from oven ▬ ▬ ▬ ▬ ▬ ➤

> **1 tablespoon margarine or butter**

3 Shake in plastic bag until mixed ▬ ▬ ▬ ➤

> **2/3 cup Bisquick Original
> baking mix
> 1 1/2 teaspoons paprika
> 1/4 teaspoon salt
> 1/4 teaspoon pepper**

4 Shake 1 piece at a time in mixture
in plastic bag, then tap a little bit
to remove any heavy layers of
baking mix ▬ ▬ ▬ ▬ ▬ ▬ ▬ ➤

> **2 1/2- to 3 1/2-pound cut-up
> broiler-fryer chicken**

5 Put chicken pieces, skin sides down,
in pan. Bake uncovered 35 minutes.
Turn chicken pieces over, using tongs. Bake about 15 minutes longer or until
juice of chicken is no longer pink when centers of thickest pieces are cut.

*Nutrition Per Serving: Calories 290 (Calories from Fat 145); Fat 16g (Saturated 4g); Cholesterol 85mg;
Sodium 370mg; Carbohydrate 8g (Dietary Fiber 0g); Protein 28g*

One-Pot Spaghetti (page 120)

ONE-POT SPAGHETTI

4 to 6 servings *(photo page 119)*

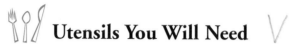 **Utensils You Will Need**

Dutch oven • Wooden spoon • Strainer • Sharp knife • Cutting board •
Can opener • Measuring spoons • Liquid measuring cup

1 Cook in Dutch oven over medium heat about 10 minutes, stirring often, until brown – – – – – – →

> **1 pound ground beef**

2 Pour beef into strainer to drain off any fat. Put beef back in Dutch oven.

3 Adult help: Wash, then chop with sharp knife – – – – – – →

> **1 medium onion**

4 Stir into beef – – – – – – →

> **The chopped onion**
> **2 cups water**
> **1 can (8 ounces) tomato sauce**
> **1 jar or can (14 to 15 ounces)**
> **spaghetti sauce with mushrooms**
> **1 teaspoon sugar**
> **1/2 teaspoon salt**

5 Add to beef mixture – – – – – – →

> **1 package (7 ounces) long**
> **spaghetti**

6 Heat beef mixture to boiling over medium-high heat, stirring a few times to to keep spaghetti from sticking. Turn heat down to low. Cover and simmer about 15 minutes or until spaghetti is tender. Remove from heat and stir once.

7 Just before serving, sprinkle with ━ ➤ | **3 tablespoons grated Parmesan cheese**

Nutrition Per Serving: Calories 535 (Calories from Fat 200); Fat 22g (Saturated 8g); Cholesterol 65mg; Sodium 1410mg; Carbohydrate 57g (Dietary Fiber 4g); Protein 31g

HINT
1 envelope (about 1 1/2 ounces) spaghetti sauce mix and 1 1/4 cups more water can be used in place of the spaghetti sauce with mushrooms.

SLEEP OVER

What fun to have friends over to spend the night and play games, watch videos, cool off with the hose or share stories. Whatever the activities, the hungries usually hit several times when kids are together. Here are some recipes to spread out during the day to cover all the bases. The crackers and spread can be eaten for an afternoon snack, the fish sticks and coleslaw for supper and the fizz for an evening snack. Follow the Easy Plan, and you and your friends will never get the "growlies."

Menu

Easy Cheesy Spread page 59

Crackers

Fish Stick Fondue page 129

Coleslaw

Pineapple Fizz page 73

Easy Game Plan

1 Several days before the sleep over, make up a shopping list from the menu and recipes and buy the ingredients that you need.

2 The morning of the sleep over, make or buy your favorite coleslaw. Make the Easy Cheesy Spread.

3 At suppertime, make the Fish Stick Fondue.

4 For the evening snack, make enough recipes of the Pineapple Fizz for everyone to have one.

Easy Cheesy Spread, Fish Stick Fondue

POLKA-DOTTED MAC
▲▲▲▲▲ AND CHEESE ▲▲▲▲▲

4 servings

Utensils You Will Need

Cutting board • Sharp knife • 3-quart saucepan • Wooden spoon • Colander •
2-quart casserole with lid • Can opener • Liquid measuring cup •
Measuring spoon • Pot holders

1 Heat oven to 375°.

2 Adult help: Cut into very thin slices, then set aside - - - - - ➤

2 hot dogs

3 Cook in saucepan as directed on package, then pour into colander to drain - - - - - ➤

1 package (7 ounces) elbow macaroni

4 Put macaroni in casserole.

5 Stir into macaroni - - - - - ➤

1 can (11 ounces) condensed Cheddar cheese soup 1/2 cup milk 1 teaspoon Worcestershire sauce

6 Put hot dog slices over top of macaroni mixture. Bake about 25 minutes or until mixture is hot and bubbly.

To Microwave:

Follow recipe above through step 5. Cover with the lid and microwave on High (100%) 3 minutes. Carefully remove lid and stir. Put hot dog slices over top of macaroni mixture. Replace lid and microwave on High (100%) 3 to 4 minutes or until hot.

Nutrition Per Serving: Calories 360 (Calories from Fat 125); Fat 14g (Saturated 7g); Cholesterol 30mg; Sodium 860mg; Carbohydrate 47g (Dietary Fiber 2g); Protein 13g

When Maggie tested this recipe she thought it would be a lot faster if it was heated in the microwave. We agree, Maggie, and have added microwave directions.

EASY THREE-CHEESE
▲▲▲▲▲ LASAGNE ▲▲▲▲▲

8 servings *(photo page 128)*

Utensils You Will Need

Medium bowl • Wooden spoon • Dry-ingredient measuring cups •
Measuring spoons • Rectangular baking dish, 12 × 7 1/2 × 2 inches •
Liquid measuring cup • Pot holders

1 Heat oven to 350°.

2 Mix in medium bowl with wooden spoon ━ ━ ━ ━ ━ ➤

> **1 container (15 ounces) ricotta cheese**
> **1/4 cup chopped fresh parsley or 2 tablespoons dried parsley flakes**
> **2 tablespoons grated Parmesan cheese**
> **1 teaspoon dried basil leaves**
> **1/2 teaspoon garlic powder**

3 To assemble lasagne, you will need ━ ➤

> **4 cups (32 ounces) spaghetti sauce**
> **8 uncooked lasagne noodles**

4 Spread 1 1/3 cups of the spaghetti sauce evenly over bottom of rectangular baking dish. Top with 4 of the noodles.

5 Spread 1 cup of the ricotta cheese mixture over noodles, then sprinkle with **half** of ━ ━ ━ ━ ━ ━ ━ ➤

> **2 cups shredded mozzarella cheese (8 ounces)**

6 Spread 1 1/3 cups of the spaghetti sauce over the mozzarella cheese.

7 Make more layers with 4 lasagne noodles, 1 cup ricotta cheese mixture and 1 1/3 cups spaghetti sauce. (Be sure spaghetti sauce completely covers noodles.) Sprinkle with the rest of the mozzarella cheese.

8 Bake uncovered 40 to 45 minutes or until noodles are tender. **Adult help:** Carefully remove pan from oven. It will be very hot and heavy. Let cool 15 minutes before cutting.

To Microwave:

Follow recipe above, using rectangular microwavable dish, 10 × 6 × 1 1/2 inches— except do not sprinkle with the last 1 cup of mozzarella cheese.

Cover dish with plastic wrap. Turn back 1 corner to make a little space for the steam to come out. Microwave on High (100%) 10 minutes. Turn dish 1/2 turn.

Microwave on Medium (50%) 22 to 28 minutes or until noodles are tender. Carefully remove plastic wrap (it will be very hot). Sprinkle with the rest of the mozzarella cheese. Cover the lasagne and let stand 15 minutes.

Nutrition Per Serving: Calories 350 (Calories from Fat 135); Fat 15g (Saturated 7g); Cholesterol 35mg; Sodium 1010mg; Carbohydrate 37g (Dietary Fiber 3g); Protein 19g

▲▲▲▲ FISH STICK FONDUE ▲▲▲▲

6 servings

🍴 Utensils You Will Need

Sharp knife • Cutting board • Cookie sheet • 2 small bowls • Dry-ingredient measuring cup • Measuring spoons • Spoon • Spatula • Serving platter • Toothpicks

1 Heat oven as directed on fish stick package.

2 Let stand at room temperature 10 minutes ▸

2 packages (8 ounces each) frozen breaded fish sticks

3 Cut each fish stick crosswise into 3 equal pieces. Put the fish pieces on cookie sheet.

4 Adult help: Chop into small pieces, then put in small bowl ▸

1 large dill pickle

5 Stir in ▸

1/2 cup mayonnaise or salad dressing
1/2 teaspoon onion powder

6 Mix in another small bowl with spoon ▸

1/2 cup chili sauce
1 teaspoon prepared horseradish
1 teaspoon lemon juice
1/4 teaspoon Worcestershire sauce

7 Bake the fish pieces as directed on package. Remove fish pieces to serving platter, using spatula. To serve, poke toothpicks into fish pieces, then dunk fish in the dips.

8 Or, if you like, serve fish pieces with ▸

Pretzel sticks

Nutrition Per Serving: Calories 330 (Calories from Fat 200); Fat 22g (Saturated 3g); Cholesterol 30mg; Sodium 1060mg; Carbohydrate 25g (Dietary Fiber 1g); Protein 9g

Easy Three-Cheese Lasagne (page 126)

▲▲▲▲▲ BAKED POTATOES ▲▲▲▲▲

4 servings

 **Utensils You Will Need**

Brush • Fork • Pot holders

1 Heat oven to 375°.

2 Scrub – – – – – – – – – – – ➤ | **4 medium potatoes** |

3 If you like, to give the potatoes softer skins, rub potatoes with – – ➤ | **Shortening** |

4 Poke potatoes with fork 2 or 3 times on top and bottom so steam can come out.

5 Bake potatoes 1 to 1 1/4 hours or until potatoes are soft enough to easily pierce with a fork.

To Microwave:

Choose 4 potatoes that are close to the same shape and size. Poke potatoes with fork 2 or 3 times on top and bottom so steam can come out.

Put potatoes about 2 inches apart in a circle on microwavable paper towel in microwave oven. Microwave uncovered on High (100%) 11 to 13 minutes or until potatoes are soft enough to easily pierce with a fork. Let potatoes stand uncovered 5 minutes before serving.

Nutrition Per Serving: Calories 90 (Calories from Fat 0); Fat 0g (Saturated 0g); Cholesterol 0mg; Sodium 5mg; Carbohydrate 20g (Dietary Fiber 1g); Protein 2g

▲▲▲▲ MASHED POTATOES ▲▲▲▲

4 servings

Utensils You Will Need

Vegetable peeler • Sharp knife • Cutting board • 3-quart saucepan •
Potato masher • Pot holders • Liquid measuring cup • Measuring spoons

1 Wash, then peel skins from ▬ ▬ ▬ ➤ | **2 pounds potatoes (about 6 medium)**

2 Adult help: Cut potatoes into large pieces with sharp knife.

3 Heat to boiling in saucepan ▬ ▬ ▬ ➤ | **1 inch water**

4 Add potatoes. Cover and heat to boiling. Turn heat down a little and boil 20 to 25 minutes.

5 Drain potatoes. Shake the saucepan gently over low heat to dry the potatoes.

6 Mash potatoes with potato masher until no lumps remain.

7 Mix in, a little at a time, with potato masher ▬ ▬ ▬ ▬ ▬ ➤ | **1/3 to 1/2 cup milk**

8 Add to potatoes, then mix with potato masher until potatoes are light and fluffy ▬ ▬ ▬ ▬ ➤ | **1/4 cup (1/2 stick) margarine or butter** **1/2 teaspoon salt** **Dash of pepper**

9 If you like, top with small amounts of ▬ ▬ ▬ ▬ ▬ ▬ ➤ | **Margarine or butter** **Paprika**

Here's another idea... Make **Parsley Mashed Potatoes:** Add 2 tablespoons chopped fresh parsley in step 8.

Nutrition Per Serving: Calories 280 (Calories from Fat 110); Fat 12g (Saturated 3g); Cholesterol 2mg; Sodium 420mg; Carbohydrate 42g (Dietary Fiber 3g); Protein 4g

BUTTERED CARROT ▲▲▲▲▲ NUGGETS ▲▲▲▲▲

4 servings

 **Utensils You Will Need**

Vegetable peeler • Sharp knife • Cutting board • 2-quart saucepan • Measuring spoons • Fork • Slotted spoon • Serving dish

1 Adult help: Wash and peel, then cut into 1/2-inch pieces with sharp knife ▪ ▪ ▪ ▪ ▪ ▪ ▪ ▪ ➤ | **6 medium carrots (about 1 pound)**

2 Pour into saucepan ▪ ▪ ▪ ▪ ▪ ➤ | **1 inch water**

3 Add carrots and ▪ ▪ ▪ ▪ ▪ ▪ ➤ | **1/4 teaspoon salt**

4 Cover and heat to boiling. Turn heat down to medium. Cook 14 to 16 minutes or until carrots are tender when poked with a fork. Remove carrots to serving dish, using slotted spoon.

5 Stir into carrots ▪ ▪ ▪ ▪ ▪ ▪ ▪ ➤ | **1 tablespoon margarine or butter**

To Microwave:

Put 1/4 cup water, the salt and carrots in microwavable 1-quart casserole or bowl. Cover casserole or bowl with lid or plastic wrap. If using plastic wrap, turn back 1 edge to make a little space for the steam to come out.

Microwave on High (100%) 4 minutes. Carefully remove lid, then stir. Re-cover and microwave on High (100%) 2 to 4 minutes longer or until carrots are tender when poked with a fork. Carefully drain carrots. Stir in the margarine.

Nutrition Per Serving: Calories 65 (Calories from Fat 25); Fat 3g (Saturated 1g); Cholesterol 0mg; Sodium 200mg; Carbohydrate 11g (Dietary Fiber 3g); Protein 1g

Maggie thought the carrots were done just right because they weren't too hard or too soft. She says of this recipe, "Anyone can make it; it's easy and it's fun."

▲▲▲▲▲ EASY FRUIT SALAD ▲▲▲▲▲

4 servings

Utensils You Will Need

Medium bowl • Dry-ingredient measuring cups • Measuring spoon • Wooden spoon • Can opener • Strainer • Sharp knife • Cutting board

1 Mix in medium bowl with wooden spoon - - - - - - - ➤

> 2/3 cup vanilla yogurt
> 1 tablespoon honey
> 1 tablespoon lemon juice

2 Gently stir in - - - - - - - ➤

> 1 can (11 ounces) mandarin orange segments, drained
> 1 can (8 ounces) pineapple chunks in syrup, drained
> 1 medium red apple, cored and sliced
> 1 cup seedless grapes
> 1 cup bite-size pieces salad greens, if you like

Nutrition Per Serving: Calories 175 (Calories from Fat 10); Fat 1g (Saturated 0g); Cholesterol 2mg; Sodium 25mg; Carbohydrate 43g (Dietary Fiber 3g); Protein 2g

We had written this recipe using plain yogurt but after Jessie suggested using vanilla yogurt instead, we changed our directions. Great idea, Jessie!

Easy Fruit Salad, Chunky Corn Bread (page 139)

▲▲▲▲ **FRUITY GELATIN MOLDS** ▲▲▲▲

10 servings

Utensils You Will Need

Kitchen scissors • Medium bowl • Liquid measuring cup • Wooden spoon • Colander • Small sharp knife • Dry-ingredient measuring cups • Ten 1-cup molds

1 Put in medium bowl - - - - - ▶ | **2 packages (3 ounces each) or 1 package (6 ounces) lemon-flavored gelatin**

2 Pour in, then stir to dissolve gelatin - ▶ | **1 1/2 cups boiling water**

3 Pour in - - - - - - - - ▶ | **2 cups orange juice**

4 Refrigerate gelatin mixture uncovered about 45 minutes or until partially thickened.

5 While gelatin is in the refrigerator, rinse in colander, then remove stems and cut in half - - - - ▶ | **1 pint strawberries**

6 Gently stir into gelatin mixture - - ▶ | **The strawberry halves 2 cups honeydew melon balls or cubes**

7 Pour gelatin mixture into molds. Refrigerate uncovered about 2 hours or until firm.

8 Unmold gelatin and, if you like, serve with - - - - - - - - →

> **1/2 cup honeydew melon balls or cubes**
> **Salad greens**

Nutrition Per Serving: Calories 110 (Calories from Fat 0); Fat 0g (Saturated 0g); Cholesterol 0mg; Sodium 45mg; Carbohydrate 26g (Dietary Fiber 1g); Protein 2g

Katie likes to make gelatin and thought these fun-shaped gelatins "tasted real good with all the fruit." Her mom suggests trying different flavors of gelatin.

▲▲▲▲ WHITE RICE ▲▲▲▲

6 servings

Utensils You Will Need

2-quart saucepan • Dry-ingredient measuring cup • Liquid measuring cup • Measuring spoon • Fork

1 Heat to boiling in saucepan, stirring once or twice - - - - - - →

> **1 cup uncooked regular long grain rice**
> **2 cups water**
> **1/2 teaspoon salt, if you like**

2 Reduce heat to low. Cover and simmer 14 minutes. (Do not lift cover or stir.) Remove saucepan from heat.

3 Fluff rice lightly with fork. Cover and let stand 5 to 10 minutes to steam.

Here's another idea…Make **Lemon Rice:** Stir 2 tablespoons margarine or butter, melted, and 2 teaspoons lemon juice into cooked rice.

Here's another idea…Make **Parsley Rice:** Stir 2 tablespoons chopped fresh parsley into cooked rice.

Nutrition Per Serving: Calories 115 (Calories from Fat 0); Fat 0g (Saturated 0g); Cholesterol 0mg; Sodium 0mg; Carbohydrate 27g (Dietary Fiber 0g); Protein 2g

Dan passed margarine and lemon juice when he served the rice to his family. He also thought it would be good with chicken chow mein instead of the usual crispy noodles.

▲▲▲▲▲ CHUNKY CORN BREAD ▲▲▲▲▲

12 servings *(photo page 135)*

Utensils You Will Need

Square pan, 8 × 8 × 2 inches • Pastry brush • Large bowl • Wooden spoon • Dry-ingredient measuring cups • Liquid measuring cup • Measuring spoons • Can opener • Pot holders • Toothpick

1 Heat oven to 400°.

2 Grease square pan with ⇢

Shortening

3 Beat in large bowl with wooden spoon until smooth ⇢

1 cup cornmeal
1 cup all-purpose flour
1 cup milk
1/4 cup vegetable oil
1 tablespoon sugar
2 teaspoons baking powder
1 teaspoon salt
2 large eggs

4 Stir in ⇢

1/2 cup drained canned whole kernel corn

5 Spread batter in pan. Bake about 25 minutes or until light brown and toothpick poked in center comes out clean. Serve warm.

Nutrition Per Serving: Calories 145 (Calories from Fat 55); Fat 6g (Saturated 1g); Cholesterol 35mg; Sodium 300mg; Carbohydrate 20g (Dietary Fiber 1g); Protein 4g

5

Anytime Desserts and Sweets

Chocolate Chip Cookies (page 155),
Mini Elephant Ears (page 162)

CHOCOLATE MALT CAKES

12 cakes

Utensils You Will Need

Muffin pan with medium cups, 2 1/2 × 1 1/4 inches, or rectangular pan, 13 × 9 × 2 inches • Medium bowl • Dry-ingredient measuring cups • Measuring spoons • Wooden spoon • Small bowl • Liquid measuring cup • Wire whisk • Pot holders • Toothpick • Wire cooling rack • Straws • Kitchen scissors • Ice-cream scoop

1 Heat oven to 350°.

2 Put in muffin cups or pan - - - - →

> **12 to 16 ice-cream cones with flat bottoms**

3 Mix in medium bowl with wooden spoon - - - - - - →

> **1 1/4 cups all-purpose flour**
> **3/4 cup sugar**
> **1/3 cup malted milk powder, if you like**
> **1/4 cup cocoa**
> **1 teaspoon baking soda**
> **1/4 teaspoon salt**

4 Mix in small bowl with wire whisk - →

> **1/4 cup vegetable oil**
> **1 teaspoon vinegar**
> **1/2 teaspoon vanilla**

5 Stir hard into flour mixture with wire whisk about 1 minute or until well mixed - - - - - - - →

> **The oil mixture**
> **2/3 cup cold water**

6 Immediately pour batter into cones, filling each to within about 1 inch of top of cone.

7 Bake about 30 minutes or until toothpick poked in centers of cakes comes out clean. Adult help: Remove cones from muffin cups or pans to wire rack. Cool completely.

8 Top each cake with small scoop of, then freeze until ready to serve ▪ ▪ ▪ ▪ ▪ ➤

> **Chocolate or vanilla ice cream**

9 Just before serving, cut in half, then poke closed ends into ice cream ▪ ▪ ▪ ▪ ➤

> **12 to 16 candy powder straws or plastic straws**

10 Squirt each "malt" with desired amount of whipped cream and top with cherry ▪ ▪ ▪ ▪ ▪ ▪ ▪ ▪ ➤

> **1 can (7 ounces) whipped cream topping**
> **12 to 16 maraschino cherries**

Nutrition Per Cake: Calories 285 (Calories from Fat 110); Fat 12g (Saturated 5g); Cholesterol 20mg; Sodium 200mg; Carbohydrate 41g (Dietary Fiber 1g); Protein 4g

Jessie liked the taste of chocolate in these fun cakes-in-a-cone. We think they make a great party treat.

▲▲▲▲ DINOSAUR CAKES ▲▲▲▲

14 cakes

Utensils You Will Need

Jelly roll pan, 15 1/2 ×10 1/2 ×1 inch • Pastry brush • Large bowl •
Dry-ingredient measuring cups • Measuring spoons • Liquid measuring cup •
Electric mixer • Rubber scraper • Fork • Pot holders • Toothpick •
Wire cooling rack • Dinosaur-shaped cookie cutters • Spatula

1 Heat oven to 350°.

2 Grease jelly roll pan with — — — ▶ | **Shortening**

3 Put small amount in pan and shake to coat, then pour out any extra — — ▶ | **All-purpose flour**

4 Beat in large bowl with electric mixer on low speed 30 seconds, scraping bowl all the time — — — — — ▶ |
2 1/3 cups all-purpose flour
1 1/3 cups sugar
1/2 cup shortening
1 1/4 cups orange juice
3 1/2 teaspoons baking powder
1 teaspoon vanilla
1/2 teaspoon salt
3 large eggs

5 Beat batter with electric mixer on high speed 3 minutes, scraping bowl a few times.

6 Add — — — — — — — ▶ | **1/4 cup multicolored candy decorations**

7 Beat batter on low speed a few seconds to mix in candy decorations. Pour batter into pan, spreading batter to corners.

8 Bake 20 to 25 minutes or until toothpick poked in center comes out clean. Cool completely on wire rack.

9 Freeze cake uncovered about 1 hour. Cut cake into dinosaur shapes with cookie cutters. Remove dinosaur cakes from pan with spatula.

10 Frost tops of cakes with frosting and sprinkle with dinosaur candies from ➤

1 tub (1 lb) chocolate ready-to-spread frosting with dinosaur candy bit sprinkles

Here's another idea…Make **Shaped Cakes:** Cut cake into shapes using your favorite cookie cutters and frost with any ready-to-spread frosting with candy bit sprinkles.

Nutrition Per Cake: Calories 390 (Calories from Fat 145); Fat 16g (Saturated 8g); Cholesterol 45mg; Sodium 210mg; Carbohydrate 59g (Dietary Fiber 1g); Protein 4g

Rachel was proud to serve her family these cute cut-out cakes that she had made herself, and she especially liked putting the candy sprinkles on top.

▲▲▲▲▲ BIG BURGER CAKE ▲▲▲▲▲

12 servings *(photo page 148)*

🍴 Utensils You Will Need

1 1/2-quart casserole • Pastry brush • Small bowl • Electric mixer •
Rubber scraper • Toothpicks • Wire cooling rack • Serving plate • Cookie sheet •
Ruler • Long serrated knife • Spatula • Small bowl • Spoon

1 Heat oven to 300°.

2 Grease casserole with ▬ ▬ ▬ ▬ ▬ ▬ ➤ | **Shortening** |

3 Put small amount in casserole and
shake to coat, then pour out any
extra ▬ ▬ ▬ ▬ ▬ ▬ ▬ ▬ ▬ ➤ | **All-purpose flour** |

4 Make as directed on package—except
pour batter into casserole ▬ ▬ ▬ ▬ ➤ | **1 package (1 lb) golden pound cake mix** |

5 Bake 1 hour 5 minutes to 1 hour 10
minutes or until toothpick poked in
center comes out clean. Cool cake on wire
rack 10 minutes. Adult help: Remove cake
from casserole and put rounded side up
on serving plate.

6 Make ▬ ▬ ▬ ▬ ▬ ▬ ▬ ▬ ▬ ▬ ➤ | **Easy Penuche Frosting (page 149)** |

7 Adult help: Mark the cake for easier cutting by sticking toothpicks in the cake to guide the knife, as shown in the drawing. Put 1 row of toothpicks (about 2 inches apart) 1 inch from the bottom of the cake and another row 2 inches from the bottom. Using toothpicks as a guide, cut the cake into 3 equal parts: 1 part for the top of the bun, 1 part for the hamburger and 1 part for the bottom of the bun.

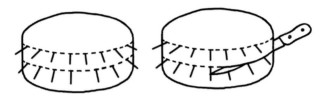

8 Frost the bottom layer with some of the Easy Penuche Frosting.

9 Measure 1/3 cup of the rest of the frosting into a bowl, then stir in ▬ ▬ ➤ | **2 tablespoons cocoa**

10 If the cocoa-flavored frosting seems stiff, stir in 1/2 teaspoon water. Put the middle (hamburger) layer on top of the frosted bottom layer. Frost the middle layer with the cocoa-flavored frosting. Put the top (rounded) layer on top of the middle layer. Frost with remaining frosting.

11 Drizzle side of middle layer with ▬ ▬ ➤ | **2 tablespoons strawberry preserves (to look like ketchup)**

12 Sprinkle top of cake with ▬ ▬ ▬ ▬ ➤ | **1 tablespoon sesame seed**

Nutrition Per Serving: Calories 410 (Calories from Fat 115); Fat 13g (Saturated 3g); Cholesterol 35mg; Sodium 370mg; Carbohydrate 71g (Dietary Fiber 1g); Protein 3g

▲▲▲▲▲ EASY PENUCHE FROSTING ▲▲▲▲▲

12 servings (About 2 cups frosting)

Utensils You Will Need

Square pan, 8 × 8 × 2 inches • 2-quart saucepan • Wooden spoon •
Dry-ingredient measuring cup • Liquid measuring cup

1 Fill square pan about 1/3 of the way to the top with cold water and ice cubes.

2 Melt in saucepan over low heat, stirring a few times - - - - - - ➤ | **1/2 cup (1 stick) margarine or butter**

3 Stir in, then cook over low heat 2 minutes, stirring a few times - - - ➤ | **1 cup packed brown sugar**

4 Stir in - - - - - - - - - ➤ | **1/4 cup milk**

5 Heat to rolling boil, stirring all the time. Remove saucepan from heat, then put it in the pan of cold water and ice.

6 Adult help: When you can comfortably hold your hand on the bottom of the saucepan, gradually stir in - - - - - - - - - ➤ | **2 cups powdered sugar**

7 Put the saucepan back in the pan of ice water. Beat the sugar mixture with wooden spoon until it becomes thick enough to spread. If the frosting is too thin, add a little more powdered sugar. If it is too thick, add a few drops of hot water.

Nutrition Per Serving: Calories 225 (Calories from Fat 70); Fat 8g (Saturated 2g); Cholesterol 0mg; Sodium 100mg; Carbohydrate 38g (Dietary Fiber 0g); Protein 0g

Big Burger Cake (page 146)

JACK-O'-LANTERN CAKE

12 servings

Utensils You Will Need

2 round pans, 9×1 1/2 or 8×1 1/2 inches • Pastry brush • Liquid measuring cup • Large bowl • Electric mixer • Pot holders • Wire cooling rack • Long spatula • Serving plate

1 Heat oven to 350°.

2 Grease round pans with ----→ **Shortening**

3 Put small amount in each pan and shake to coat, then pour out any extra ----→ **All-purpose flour**

4 Make and bake as directed on package, dividing batter between the 2 pans ----→ **1 package (1 lb 2.25 oz) spice or carrot cake mix with pudding**

5 Adult help: Cool cakes in pans 10 minutes, then remove from pans to wire rack. Cool completely.

6 Make ----→ **Creamy Frosting (page 151)**

7 Tint frosting orange by stirring in a few drops of red and yellow food colors. Start with just 1 or 2 drops, adding more drops to get the color of orange you like. Put 1 cake, rounded side down, on a plate. Spread some of the frosting over the top of the cake. Top with second cake, rounded side up. Frost the side and top of the cake.

8 Make a jack-o'-lantern face on cake with ----→ **Flat black jelly candies
Candy corn**

Nutrition Per Serving: Calories 435 (Calories from Fat 155); Fat 17g (Saturated 3g); Cholesterol 55mg; Sodium 380mg; Carbohydrate 68g (Dietary Fiber 0g); Protein 3g

▲▲▲▲▲ CREAMY FROSTING ▲▲▲▲▲

12 servings (About 2 cups frosting)

Utensils You Will Need

Medium bowl • Wooden spoon • Dry-ingredient measuring cups •
Small sharp knife • Measuring spoons

1 Mix in medium bowl with
wooden spoon ▬ ▬ ▬ ▬ ▬ ▬ ▶

> **3 cups powdered sugar**
> **1/3 cup (from a stick) margarine**
> **or butter, softened**

2 Stir in ▬ ▬ ▬ ▬ ▬ ▬ ▶

> **2 tablespoons milk**
> **1 1/2 teaspoons vanilla**

3 Beat frosting with wooden spoon until smooth and spreadable. If frosting is
too thin, add a little more powdered sugar. If frosting is too
thick, add a few drops of milk.

*Nutrition Per Serving: Calories 165 (Calories from Fat 45); Fat 5g
(Saturated 1g); Cholesterol 0mg; Sodium 60mg;
Carbohydrate 30g (Dietary Fiber 0g); Protein 0g*

HINT
*Frosting is best
when it's creamy
and smooth but
still holds its
shape.*

FROZEN CHOCOLATE ▲▲▲▲▲ CRUNCH ▲▲▲▲▲

4 servings

 **Utensils You Will Need**

Medium bowl • Eggbeater • Liquid measuring cup • Measuring spoons •
Rubber scraper • 4 small dessert bowls or custard cups

1 Chill medium bowl in freezer about 15 minutes or until cold.

2 Beat in chilled bowl with eggbeater until stiff ▶

> **1 cup whipping (heavy) cream**
> **1/3 cup chocolate-flavored syrup**

3 Gently stir into whipped cream with rubber scraper ▶

> **2 tablespoons almond brickle chips**
> **1 teaspoon vanilla**

4 Divide mixture equally among dessert bowls. Freeze uncovered about 2 hours or until firm.

5 Sprinkle with candy decorations just before serving if you like.

Nutrition Per Serving: Calories 265 (Calories from Fat 180); Fat 20g (Saturated 13g); Cholesterol 65mg; Sodium 50mg; Carbohydrate 20g (Dietary Fiber 1g); Protein 2g

HINT

If Frozen Chocolate Crunch freezes too hard, just set it out at room temperature about 5 minutes to soften a little before serving.

Frozen Chocolate Crunch, Fantastic Fudge (page 159)

OH-SO-CHOCOLATE ▲▲▲▲▲ BROWNIES ▲▲▲▲▲

36 brownies

Utensils You Will Need

Rectangular pan, 13 × 9 × 2 inches • Pastry brush • 2-quart saucepan • Wooden spoon • Dry-ingredient measuring cups • Measuring spoons • Rubber scraper • Pot holders • Wire cooling rack • Sharp knife

1 Heat oven to 350°.

2 Grease rectangular pan with - - - → **Shortening**

3 Melt in saucepan over low heat, stirring a few times, then remove from heat - - - - - - - - - - →

**4 ounces unsweetened chocolate
2/3 cup shortening**

4 Stir in - - - - - - - - - - →

**2 cups granulated sugar
1 teaspoon vanilla
4 large eggs**

5 Stir in - - - - - - - - - - →

6 Spread batter in pan. Bake 30 minutes or until brownies start to pull away from sides of pan. Do not overbake!

**1 1/4 cups all-purpose flour
1 cup chopped nuts
1 teaspoon baking powder
1/2 teaspoon salt**

7 Cool the brownies slightly on wire rack. Cut into 2 × 1 1/2-inch bars. Cool completely.

8 Sprinkle with - - - - - - - - - - → **Powdered sugar**

Nutrition Per Brownie: Calories 145 (Calories from Fat 70); Fat 8g (Saturated 2g); Cholesterol 25mg; Sodium 50mg; Carbohydrate 17g (Dietary Fiber 1g); Protein 2g

CHOCOLATE CHIP COOKIES

About 24 cookies

Utensils You Will Need

Large bowl • Wooden spoon • Dry-ingredient measuring cups • Measuring spoons • Tablespoon • Cookie sheet • Pot holders • Spatula • Wire cooling rack

1 Heat oven to 375°.

2 Mix in large bowl with wooden spoon ----->
> 1/2 cup granulated sugar
> 1/2 cup packed brown sugar
> 1/2 cup (1 stick) margarine or butter, softened
> 1 large egg

3 Stir in ----->
> 1 1/2 cups all-purpose flour
> 1/2 teaspoon baking soda
> 1/2 teaspoon salt

4 Stir in ----->
> 1 package (6 ounces) semisweet chocolate chips (1 cup)
> 1/2 cup chopped nuts

5 Drop dough by rounded table-spoonfuls onto cookie sheet. Bake 10 to 12 minutes or until light brown.

6 Cool cookies on cookie sheet 1 minute, then remove with spatula to wire rack. Cool.

Here's another idea…Make **Cookies-on-a-Stick:** Poke 1 ice cream stick into the side of each drop of dough until tip of stick is in center of dough.

Here's another idea…Make **Colorful Candy Cookies:** Use 1 cup candy-coated chocolate candies, in place of the chocolate chips.

Nutrition Per Cookie: Calories 150 (Calories from Fat 70); Fat 8g (Saturated 2g); Cholesterol 10mg; Sodium 120mg; Carbohydrate 20g (Dietary Fiber 1g); Protein 1g

▲▲▲▲▲ BLACK-EYED SUSANS ▲▲▲▲▲

About 36 cookies *(photo page 158)*

Utensils You Will Need

Small sharp knife • Large bowl • Dry-ingredient measuring cups • Measuring spoons • Wooden spoon • Plastic wrap • Ruler • Cookie sheet • Kitchen scissors • Pot holders • Spatula • Wire cooling rack

1 Mix in large bowl with wooden spoon ----------→

> 3/4 cup (1 1/2 sticks) margarine or butter, softened
> 1/2 cup sugar
> 1 teaspoon vanilla
> 12 drops yellow food color
> 1 large egg
> 1 package (3 ounces) cream cheese, softened

2 Stir in ----------→

> 2 cups all-purpose flour

3 Cover dough with plastic wrap and refrigerate about 2 hours or until firm.

4 Heat oven to 375°.

5 Shape dough into 1 1/4-inch balls. Put balls about 2 inches apart on cookie sheet. As you put each ball on the cookie sheet, cut it following the directions in step 6.

6 Adult help: Using scissors or a small, sharp knife, cut each ball from top into 6 wedges about 3/4 of the way through dough, as shown in drawing. Spread wedges apart slightly. (Cookies will flatten as they bake.)

7 Bake 10 to 12 minutes or until cookies are set and edges begin to brown.

8 Immediately press in center of each cookie 1 of ----------> | **36 chocolate stars** |

9 Remove cookies from cookie sheet with spatula to wire rack. Cool.

Nutrition Per Cookie: Calories 100 (Calories from Fat 55); Fat 6g (Saturated 2g); Cholesterol 10mg; Sodium 55mg; Carbohydrate 10g (Dietary Fiber 0g); Protein 1g

Besides liking to eat these pretty flower-shaped cookies, Jenna says, "It was fun to cut the shapes and put in the chocolate stars."

▲▲▲▲▲ FANTASTIC FUDGE ▲▲▲▲▲

About 64 pieces

 **Utensils You Will Need**

Square pan, 8 × 8 × 2 inches • 2-quart saucepan • Wooden spoon •
Can opener • Measuring spoons

1 Grease square pan with ‑ ‑ ‑ ‑ ‑ ‑ ➤ | **Margarine or butter**

2 Melt in saucepan over low heat, stirring
a few times, then remove from heat ‑ ➤ | **1 package (12 ounces) and
1 package (6 ounces) semisweet
chocolate chips (3 cups)**

3 Stir in ‑ ‑ ‑ ‑ ‑ ‑ ‑ ‑ ‑ ‑ ‑ ➤ | **1 can (14 ounces) sweetened
condensed milk
1 teaspoon vanilla
Dash of salt**

4 Pour chocolate mixture into pan.
Spread evenly with the back of a spoon. Refrigerate uncovered about 2 hours
or until firm. Cut fudge into 1-inch squares. Cover and refrigerate any leftover fudge.

5 If you like, decorate squares of fudge to look like dice by making dots on top
with white decorating icing.

Here's another idea…Make **Fantastic Nutty Fudge:** Stir 1/2 to 3/4 cup chopped nuts into
melted chocolate.

*Nutrition Per Piece: Calories 60 (Calories from Fat 25); Fat 3g (Saturated 2g); Cholesterol 2mg; Sodium 15mg;
Carbohydrate 8g (Dietary Fiber 1g); Protein 1g*

Black-eyed Susans (page 156)

HALLOWEEN PARTY

Treat your friends to a fun-filled event on the spookiest day of the year with these perfect-for-Halloween foods. Your friends won't play any tricks on you after eating this yummy menu. Save the seeds from your jack-o'-lantern and toast them in the oven for a crunchy munchy. Follow the Easy Plan and pulling this party together won't be the least bit scary.

Menu

Candy Corn

Fiesta Chili page 112

Chunky Corn Bread page 139

Toasted Pumpkin Seeds

Jack-O'-Lantern Cake page 150

Orange Soda

Easy Party Plan

1 Several days before the party, make up a shopping list from the menu and recipes and buy the ingredients that you need.

2 Two days before, carve a pumpkin and toast the seeds, if you like. Store the pumpkin outside in the cool weather and don't burn a candle in it until the party.

3 The day before, bake the cake for the Jack-O'-Lantern Cake. Bake the Chunky Corn Bread while the oven is still on.

4 The morning of the party, assemble and decorate the cake.

5 About an hour before the party, start making the Fiesta Chili. Reheat the corn bread at 300° for 10 minutes just before serving.

▲▲▲▲▲ MINI ELEPHANT EARS ▲▲▲▲▲

About 48 cookies

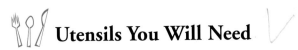 **Utensils You Will Need**

Cookie sheet • Pastry brush • Rolling pin • Ruler • Sharp knife • Dry-ingredient measuring cup • Small bowl • Spatula • Pot holders • Wire cooling rack

1 Heat oven to 375°.

2 Lightly grease cookie sheet with — — ➤ | **Shortening** |

3 Sprinkle a clean surface (such as a kitchen counter or breadboard) with ▪ ➤ | **Sugar** |

4 On sugared surface, roll into 12 × 9 1/2-inch rectangle that is 1/8 inch thick — — — — — ➤ | **1/2 package (17 1/4-ounce size) frozen puff pastry sheets, thawed** |

5 Adult help: Mark a line lengthwise down center of pastry rectangle. Fold long sides of rectangle toward the center line, leaving 1/4 inch uncovered at center, as shown in the drawing. Fold rectangle lengthwise in half, pressing pastry together, to form a strip, 12 × 2 1/2 inches. Cut strip crosswise into 1/4-inch slices.

6 Mix in small bowl with spoon ━ ━ ➤

> **1/2 cup sugar**
> **1 teaspoon ground cinnamon**

7 Dip slices in sugar mixture to coat both sides. Put slices about 2 inches apart on cookie sheet.

8 Bake 8 to 10 minutes, turning after 5 minutes, until cookies begin to turn golden brown. Immediately remove cookies from cookie sheet with spatula to wire rack. Cool completely.

Here's another idea... Make **Chocolate-dipped Elephant Ears:** Melt 1 ounce semisweet chocolate in 1-quart saucepan over low heat, stirring a few times. Dip ends of cookies in chocolate. Put cookies on waxed paper until chocolate is firm.

Nutrition Per Cookie: Calories 35 (Calories from Fat 20); Fat 2g (Saturated 1g); Cholesterol 0mg; Sodium 10mg; Carbohydrate 4g (Dietary Fiber 0g); Protein 0g

Leslie thought it was fun to watch the flat cookies puff in the oven as they baked. Once she made some following the directions, she started experimenting with the dough and made some smaller and some larger.

▲▲▲▲▲ CARAMEL APPLES ▲▲▲▲▲

6 apples *(photo page 166)*

Utensils You Will Need

6 round wooden sticks • Measuring spoons • Waxed paper • 1 1/2-quart saucepan • Wooden spoon • Dry-ingredient measuring cup

1 Wash and dry, then poke a wooden stick in the stem end of each of ━ ━ ━ ━ ➤

6 medium apples

2 Using 1 tablespoon for each mound, make 6 mounds about 3 inches apart on waxed paper with ━ ━ ━ ━ ➤

6 tablespoons granola or chopped peanuts

3 Heat in saucepan over low heat about 20 minutes, stirring a few times, until melted and smooth, then remove from heat ━ ━ ━ ━ ➤

**1/4 cup creamy peanut butter
3 tablespoons water
1/2 teaspoon ground cinnamon
1 package (14 ounces) vanilla caramels, unwrapped**

4 Dip apples, one at a time, in hot caramel mixture and spoon caramel over apple until it is completely coated. (If caramel thickens, heat over low heat.)

5 Hold the stick so apple is right side up for a second, then turn apple upside down and put it on one of the mounds of granola. Turn the apple so all the granola sticks to it.

6 Refrigerate apples on cookie sheet about 1 hour or until caramel coating is firm.

To Microwave:

Follow steps 1 and 2 above to prepare apples and granola. Use 2 tablespoons water in place of the 3 tablespoons water. Put water, peanut butter, cinnamon and caramels in 4-cup microwavable measuring cup.

Microwave uncovered on High (100%) 2 minutes, then stir. Microwave uncovered on High (100%) 30 to 60 seconds longer or until caramels can be stirred smooth. Finish recipe starting at step 4 above. (If caramel thickens, microwave uncovered on High (100%) 30 seconds.)

Here's another idea…Make **Chocolaty Caramel Apples:** Use 2 tablespoons water in place of the 3 tablespoons water. Use 1/4 cup chocolate chips in place of the peanut butter and chocolate caramels in place of the vanilla caramels.

Nutrition Per Apple: Calories 435 (Calories from Fat 115); Fat 13g (Saturated 7g); Cholesterol 5mg; Sodium 220mg; Carbohydrate 78g (Dietary Fiber 5g); Protein 6g

HINT
Wash and dry apples thoroughly to remove as much wax as possible.

▲▲▲▲ OVEN CARAMEL CORN ▲▲▲▲

12 cups corn

🍴 Utensils You Will Need

2 rectangular pans, 13 × 9 × 2 inches • 2-quart saucepan • Dry-ingredient measuring cup • Liquid measuring cup • Measuring spoons • Wooden spoon

1 Heat oven to 200°.

2 Divide between rectangular pans - - - ▶ | **12 cups popped popcorn (about 3/4 cup unpopped)**

3 Heat in saucepan over medium heat, stirring a few times, until bubbly around edges - - - - - - - - ▶ | **1 cup packed brown sugar**
1/2 cup (1 stick) margarine or butter
1/4 cup light corn syrup
1/2 teaspoon salt

4 Keep cooking over medium heat 5 minutes, stirring a few times.

5 Remove saucepan from heat, then stir in until foamy - - - - - - ▶ | **1/2 teaspoon baking soda**

6 Adult help: Quickly pour half the caramel mixture over popcorn in each pan, stirring until popcorn is well coated.

7 Bake 1 hour, stirring every 15 minutes. Cool.

Nutrition Per Cup: Calories 225 (Calories from Fat 110); Fat 12g (Saturated 2g); Cholesterol 0mg; Sodium 250mg; Carbohydrate 29g (Dietary Fiber 1g); Protein 1g

Leslie thinks making caramel corn is a great idea when you're bored—it's easy to do, tastes good and keeps you busy! You will want to ask an adult to help you pop the corn before you start, though.

Caramel Apples (page 164)

▲▲▲▲▲ POPCORN BALLS ▲▲▲▲▲

12 popcorn balls

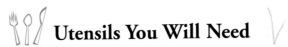 **Utensils You Will Need**

Dutch oven • Dry-ingredient measuring cups • Liquid measuring cups •
Small sharp knife • Measuring spoons • Wooden spoon • Ruler • Waxed paper •
Plastic wrap

1 Heat to boiling in Dutch oven over medium-high heat, stirring all the time with wooden spoon ▬ ▬ ▬ ▬ ▶

> **1/2 cup sugar**
> **1/4 cup (1/2 stick) margarine or butter**
> **1/2 cup light corn syrup**
> **1/2 teaspoon salt**
> **Few drops of food color, if you like**

2 Keep boiling 2 minutes, stirring all the time. Remove Dutch oven from heat.

3 Stir in until well coated ▬ ▬ ▬ ▬ ▶

> **8 cups popped popcorn (about 1/2 cup unpopped)**

4 Adult help: Cool popcorn mixture just until cool enough to handle. Shape popcorn mixture into 2-inch balls with hands dipped in cold water. Put balls on waxed paper. Cool.

5 Wrap balls individually in plastic wrap, or put each ball in a plastic bag and tie.

Nutrition Per Ball: Calories 155 (Calories from Fat 65); Fat 7g (Saturated 1g); Cholesterol 0mg; Sodium 150mg; Carbohydrate 23g (Dietary Fiber 1g); Protein 1g

Everyone loved the popcorn balls, especially Maggie's dad, and they were less messy to make than her mom thought! Although they're easy to make, Maggie says, "You really do need adult help because it is very sticky."

HINT
Don't rub your hands with margarine to shape the balls, as many older recipes suggest. The margarine can heat up too much and burn you.

▲▲▲▲▲ **TAFFY** ▲▲▲▲▲

About 48 candies

Utensils You Will Need

Square pan, 8 × 8 × 2 inches • Pastry brush • 2-quart saucepan •
Dry-ingredient measuring cups • Measuring spoons • Wooden spoon •
Liquid measuring cups • Small sharp knife • Candy thermometer • Ruler •
Kitchen scissors • Plastic wrap

1 Grease square pan with ▶ **Shortening**

2 Mix in saucepan with wooden spoon ▶ **1 cup sugar**
1 tablespoon cornstarch

3 Stir in ▶ **3/4 cup light corn syrup**
2/3 cup water
**2 tablespoons (from a stick)
margarine or butter**
1 teaspoon salt

4 Adult help: Heat sugar mixture to boiling over medium heat, stirring all the
time. Cook without stirring to 256° on candy thermometer or until a small
amount of mixture dropped into very cold water forms a hard ball that holds
its shape but can be molded. Remove
saucepan from heat.

5 Stir in ▶ **2 teaspoons vanilla**
**1/4 teaspoon food color,
if you like**

6 Pour sugar mixture into square pan.
Cool sugar mixture just until cool
enough to handle.

7 Adult help: Pull taffy with lightly buttered hands until silky, light in color and stiff. Pull taffy into long strips, 1/2 inch wide. Cut strips into 1 1/2-inch pieces with scissors.

8 Wrap pieces individually in plastic wrap or waxed paper (taffy must be wrapped to hold its shape).

To Microwave:

Grease square pan as directed. Mix sugar and cornstarch in microwavable 2-quart casserole. Stir in remaining ingredients except vanilla and food color. Microwave uncovered on High (100%) 5 minutes, then stir.

Microwave 12 to 16 minutes longer to 256° on microwave candy thermometer or until a small amount of mixture dropped into very cold water forms a hard ball that holds its shape but can be molded. Stir in vanilla and food color. Finish recipe starting at step 6 above.

Here's another idea…Make **Peppermint Taffy:** Use 1 tablespoon peppermint extract in place of the vanilla. Stir in 1/4 teaspoon red food color with the peppermint extract.

Nutrition Per Candy: Calories 35 (Calories from Fat 0); Fat 0g (Saturated 0g); Cholesterol 0mg; Sodium 55mg; Carbohydrate 8g (Dietary Fiber 0g); Protein 0g

Max says that if you want to chew for a long time, this is your recipe! He thought it was hard to tell when the sugar mixture was ready. We agree that it can be difficult for the beginning candy maker and think a candy thermometer is very helpful.

METRIC CONVERSION GUIDE

VOLUME

U.S. Units	Canadian Metric	Australian Metric
1/4 teaspoon	1 mL	1 ml
1/2 teaspoon	2 mL	2 ml
1 teaspoon	5 mL	5 ml
1 tablespoon	15 mL	20 ml
1/4 cup	50 mL	60 ml
1/3 cup	75 mL	80 ml
1/2 cup	125 mL	125 ml
2/3 cup	150 mL	170 ml
3/4 cup	175 mL	190 ml
1 cup	250 mL	250 ml
1 quart	1 liter	1 liter
1 1/2 quarts	1.5 liters	1.5 liters
2 quarts	2 liters	2 liters
2 1/2 quarts	2.5 liters	2.5 liters
3 quarts	3 liters	3 liters
4 quarts	4 liters	4 liters

MEASUREMENTS

Inches	Centimeters
1	2.5
2	5.0
3	7.5
4	10.0
5	12.5
6	15.0
7	17.5
8	20.5
9	23.0
10	25.5
11	28.0
12	30.5
13	33.0
14	35.5
15	38.0

WEIGHT

U.S. Units	Canadian Metric	Australian Metric
1 ounce	30 grams	30 grams
2 ounces	55 grams	60 grams
3 ounces	85 grams	90 grams
4 ounces (1/4 pound)	115 grams	125 grams
8 ounces (1/2 pound)	225 grams	225 grams
16 ounces (1 pound)	455 grams	500 grams
1 pound	455 grams	1/2 kilogram

TEMPERATURES

Fahrenheit	Celsius
32°	0°
212°	100°
250°	120°
275°	140°
300°	150°
325°	160°
350°	180°
375°	190°
400°	200°
425°	220°
450°	230°
475°	240°
500°	260°

Note: The recipes in this cookbook have not been developed or tested using metric measures. When converting recipes to metric, some variations in quality may be noted.

Index

Page numbers in *italics* indicate photographs.